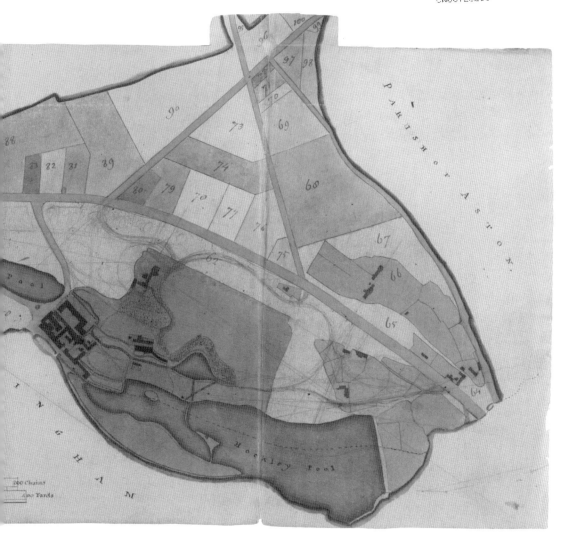

Section from Matthew Boulton's plan of his landholdings at Soho of 1793, showing his planned extensions to the existing walks on the additional land purchased in 1794-5.

A Lost Landscape

*Matthew Boulton's
Gardens at Soho*

Sketch of the Hermitage by John Phillp, 1795. The garden chair was of a type popular for indoor and outdoor use.

A LOST LANDSCAPE

Matthew Boulton's Gardens at Soho

Phillada Ballard, Val Loggie
and
Shena Mason

PHILLIMORE

2009

Published by
PHILLIMORE & CO. LTD
Chichester, West Sussex, England
www.phillimore.co.uk
www.thehistorypress.co.uk

ISBN 978-1-86077-563-5

Printed and bound in Great Britain

CONTENTS

LIST OF ILLUSTRATIONS

Frontispiece – John Phillp, sketch of the Hermitage

ACKNOWLEDGEMENTS

I n the second half of the 18th century the pioneer industrialist Matthew Boulton established extensive gardens and a landscaped park around his home and Manufactory at Soho in Handsworth, on the outskirts of Birmingham. Research into the history of these gardens and the whole of the Soho Estate was carried out by Dr Phillada Ballard and Val Loggie in the 1990s as part of the restoration and development of Boulton's home, Soho House, as a museum. Over the years since then, further inroads have been made on the mass of archival and other evidence, and the bicentenary of Matthew Boulton's death in 2009 seems an appropriate moment to present the results of all this work in detail for the first time.

It would not have been possible to publish this book without the financial and practical support of a number of organisations, and the authors acknowledge with gratitude the help of the Birmingham Common Good Trust, Birmingham Museums & Art Gallery, Birmingham Archives & Heritage Services (especially Fiona Tait and Richard Albutt), the Friends of Birmingham Museums & Art Gallery, the Firs Trust, the Hugh and Anne Kenrick Trust, Mrs Anne Kenrick and Professor E.J.T. Collins.

Illustration Acknowledgements

Figures and Colour Plates are kindly provided by courtesy of the following:

Phillada Ballard: Figs 1, 9; Birmingham Central Library, Archives & Heritage Services: Figs 2 (MS 3782/12/108/7), 4 (MS 3147/5/146a), 7 (MS 1682, Lot 38), 8 (MS 3782/6/7/346), 13 (MS 1682-81), 14 (MS 3782/12/108/70), 22 (MS 3782/12/591/211), 31 (MS 3782/13/149/42), 32 (MS 3147/5/1469), 33 (MS 3782/13/149/64), 35, 36 (BAH 369956), 37 (BAH 134251), 38 (MS 3782/21/24/8), 39 (WK/H5/535), 43 (WK/H5/646), 44, 46 (WK/H5/272), 47 (WK/H5/180), 49, 50 (WK/H5/331), Plate 7 (MS 3782/12/108/68); Birmingham Museums & Art Gallery: Frontispiece (2003.0031.11), Figs 3 (2003.0031.22), 5 (2003.0031.58), 10 (2003.0031.36), 11 (2003.0031.90), 12 (2003.0031.34), 15 (2003.0031.25), 16 (2003.0031.39), 17 (2003.0031.44), 18, 19 (2003.0031.24), 20 (2003.0031.12), 21 (2003.0031.105), 23 (2003.0031.14), 24 (2003.0031.107), 25 (2003.0031.91), 26 (2003.0031.54), 27 (2003.0031.35), 28 (2003.0031.33), 29 (2003.0031.41), 30 (2003.0031.16), 34, 40 (67'93), 48, Plates 1 (1987 F 106), 2 (2003.0031.28), 3 (2003.0031.8), 4 (2003.0031.26), 5 (2003.0031.17), 6 (2003.0031.23), 9 (2003.0031.155), 10 (2003.0031.59), 11 (2003.0031.32), 12 (2003.0031.157), 13 (1976 V 111); Shena Mason: Plates 14, 15, 16 (object in private collection); Handsworth Historical Society: Figs 41, 42, 45; The Trustees of the William Salt Library, Stafford: Plate 8 (SV VII 25a).

Introduction

'A chearfull pleasant Spot'
Matthew Boulton and Soho

Shena Mason

This is a book about a factory owner's garden. The garden (or more properly, because this was a man who thought big, the garden and park) disappeared long ago beneath successive waves of intensive inner-city development. We know it was there because two centuries and more ago people tended it, and wrote about it, and drew it and painted it, but of the land itself not much more than a pocket-handkerchief-sized plot remains uncovered, while of the actual garden nothing survives but a pair of stone sphinxes whose enigmatic gaze once surveyed its rolling expanse.

The man who planned the garden and its buildings and water features, who chose its plants and watched anxiously over its trees and picked the peaches off its sunny fruit wall, was Matthew Boulton (1728-1809), a name we associate more readily with steam engines than with gardening. One of the leading figures of the early Industrial Revolution, Matthew Boulton was responsible, with his business partner, the engineer James Watt, for developing new applications for steam power and supplying steam engines for industrial processes throughout Britain and Europe and as far afield as Australia and the Americas. As a founder-member of the Lunar Society, one of the 18th century's foremost groups of 'natural philosophers' (what we would now call scientists), he was also in at the birth of some of the most radical scientific ideas of the age of Enlightenment. His interests were wide-ranging. Viewed close-up through his microscope or at great distance through his telescope, the other worlds he encountered through the lens fired his imagination, while fossils and the geology of the ground beneath his feet set him and his friends musing about what creatures had lived here before people, and how old the earth really was (some Bibles said 6,000 years but to Boulton and his friends that was clearly preposterous, it had to be aeons older than that). With these interests in the natural sciences, it is not so surprising that one of Boulton's abiding passions was his garden at Soho House in the Parish of Handsworth, some two miles north-west from the centre of Birmingham.

Birmingham in the mid-18th century was an old-established country market town undergoing a rapid transformation into a major centre of manufacturing, chiefly in metals. When Matthew Boulton leased Soho at the age of 33, he was already gaining a reputation beyond Birmingham as man who made things happen. He had cut his business teeth in the late 1740s in his father's toy-making workshops on Snow Hill in the town centre (so-called 'Birmingham toys' were not children's playthings but small items for personal use, such as buckles, buttons, snuffboxes, vinaigrettes, chatelaines and similar articles). In 1759 Matthew Boulton's life underwent two major changes. His first wife, Mary, née Robinson, of Lichfield, died, and was followed a month later by his father, Matthew Boulton senior. The newly-widowed younger Boulton now took control of the business. The following year he remarried. The second Mrs Boulton was Mary's sister, Ann. With two wives' capital behind him (for he had 'married well' – the Robinsons were a prosperous family), Boulton set about finding a site for a much bigger factory, and in 1761 acquired the lease on 13 acres of land at Soho (the name is said to come, like that of Soho in London, from a hunting cry).

The site was mainly open heathland. A modest house, Soho House, already stood on the highest part of it (the house accounted for £300 of the £1,000 Boulton paid for the lease). The house was unfinished, but in any case it was not the main attraction of the site. The Soho land included a slitting mill (where the mill-wheel drove machinery which cut bars of metal into thin rods or strips for various uses such as nail-making). This stood at the head of a small mill pool which had been formed by damming the Hockley Brook. Boulton set about replacing the existing mill with a much larger manufactory in which water-powered machinery could be used. While this was going on he had Soho House finished off, and moved his mother and one of his sisters, probably Mary,[1] into it, while he and his second wife remained in the old family home at Snow Hill. A year or so later, when Boulton took on a business partner, John Fothergill, old Mrs Boulton and her daughter moved back into the town centre and Fothergill took up residence at Soho House. Not until 1766 did Matthew Boulton and his wife move there. Their two children were born at Soho House, Anne in 1768 and Matthew Robinson Boulton in 1770.

The building of what was to become the world-famous Soho Manufactory, a few minutes' walk from the house, took several years. Matthew Boulton's Soho, where between 600 and 1,000 people were employed, became a showpiece attracting well-to-do visitors from far and wide. These early industrial tourists came to gaze in fascination at the production processes, the division of labour which they saw in operation (an innovative idea at the time) and the sheer scale of the enterprise. Some of them were simply looking for a good day out and material for their diaries, others were bent on conducting a little manufacturing espionage.[2] The old family range of buttons and buckles was expanded to include all manner of ornamental and luxury goods in metals, including silverware, Sheffield plate, ormolu, coins and medals. Catering largely to the moneyed classes including the Royal family, the business grew and exported its wares worldwide.

But there were problems: the water supply which powered the machinery was not always reliable – in summer it sometimes dried up and in winter often froze, bringing production to a standstill. A further pool was created to increase the water flow. Much later, this would be merged with another existing pool to create the large lake which forms such a feature of contemporary images of the place. However, Boulton saw the efficient solution to the water problem in steam, and in 1774 invited James Watt to move from Scotland and join him at Soho, so that Watt could continue his development work on the steam engine. This was something which could not only keep the machines running at Soho, it was a marketable proposition. While the Soho Manufactory continued to turn out tiny items like buttons and watch-chain links, it also began to produce parts for great steam engines which were installed around the country, to pump out mines, operate mills and drive manufacturing machinery. Boulton famously observed to James Boswell during the latter's visit to Soho in 1776, 'I sell here, Sir, what all the world desires to have – POWER!'[3]

From his earliest days at Soho, Boulton took a deep interest in the garden. By adding to the original 13 acres from time to time, he gradually built up a garden and parkland of around eighty acres surrounding his house and Manufactory. The whole estate, including farmland, would eventually total over 200 acres. He read widely on the subject of landscape gardening and kept copious garden notes. These notes, along with sketches, watercolours and other archive material, provide the evidence for this book.

Though the garden at Soho was created primarily for the Boulton family's use and pleasure, it was also a statement of Matthew Boulton's own taste, intellectual interests and social aspirations. It is also clear from his notes that he saw it as a way of increasing the dramatic impact of the Manufactory, and thus as an integral part of his marketing effort. He jotted down the query, 'How shall I plant & form my Western Ground so as to be handsome to ye sight of those going to ye Manufactory?' and answered his own question with, 'Make all the Entrances into Soho Dark by plantations & enter through Gothick arches made by Trees,'[4] thus echoing the ideas of Alexander Pope who had written of 'planting trees to resemble a Gothic Cathedral'.[5] The garden was thus very much part of what might be termed the 'Soho theatre'.

It was Boulton's business to be keenly aware of prevailing fashions in all things, and essential to his image (to say nothing of his inclinations) to live in elegant and fashionable surroundings. His transformation of the estate was clearly influenced by the prevailing ideas of the landscape gardeners. Characteristically, however, he put his own stamp on those ideas. He assembled the typical landscape garden elements of woodland, lawn, meadow, flowers, shrubberies, specimen trees, water and architecture. The gardens and park which he wove from them (to the fresh air of which, a correspondent observed, 'the most wonderful effects are ascribed')[6] not only gave him, his family, friends, and occasionally the public, great pleasure, but also formed a suitably impressive backdrop for his Manufactory. The lake supplied the water he needed first for water power and later for steam power. In return, the Manufactory's steam engines supplied the power to pump water up the hill to irrigate the gardens – a symbiotic relationship, the neatness of which would undoubtedly have given Boulton great satisfaction.

Matthew Boulton died at Soho House on 17 August 1809 and his son, Matthew Robinson Boulton, inherited the estate, which he continued to develop. M.R. Boulton was especially interested in the orchard and kitchen garden and his papers contain much of interest to the historian of fruit and vegetable cultivation.

Today, Soho House is all that remains of Matthew Boulton's 'empire' at Handsworth. The house was restored by Birmingham Museums & Art Gallery and opened as a museum in 1995. With its small present garden it forms a quiet oasis in a densely built-up suburb. Matthew Boulton's cherished landscape has long since disappeared, and to reveal it we have to excavate, not on the ground but in the Matthew Boulton Papers, part of the Archives of Soho, preserved in Birmingham Archives & Heritage Services at the city's Central Library. There, and in the work of a young artist, John Phillp, who sketched and painted around the estate in the 1790s,[7] it is possible to find what cannot now be found above ground: the ambience of Soho. Amid instructions to the gardeners, nurserymen's bills and little sketches of temples, are letters which lead us into the lost gardens of Soho. One friend, Fanny de Luc, writes that she and Miss Boulton have tried the newly laid out 'Warwickshire walk' in the park, 'which was a great expedition for us both & afforded us a very great satisfaction'. That part of the garden, she adds, 'transports one in imagination to the most remote & sweet of retreats'.[8] Another friend and visitor, the astronomer Sir William Herschel, describes Soho as 'that blissful mansion' and 'your Elisium'.[9] This book, then, traces the search for Elysium, and what happened to it.

ONE

'Made from the barren wast by me'
THE SOHO LANDSCAPE, 1757-94

Phillada Ballard

On yonder gentle slope which shrubs adorn,
Where grew of late rank weeds, gorse, ling and thorn,
Now pendant woods and shady groves are seen,
And Nature there assumes a nobler mien
Here verdant lawns, cool grots, peaceful bow'rs,
Luxurient, now are strew'd with sweetest flowers,
Reflected by the Lake, which spreads below,
And Nature smiles around – there stands Soho!

This verse from James Bisset's *Magnificent Directory of Birmingham*,[1] published in 1800, describes a scene which by then had had over 30 years of effort and expense lavished on it. However, the site when Matthew Boulton acquired it in 1761 was barren and unpromising. That year he had taken over from the toymakers Edward Ruston and John Eaves the lease on 13 acres which they had been granted in 1757. This covered a slitting mill which they had built *c*.1757, together with part of its mill pool, an unfinished house, Soho House, and its immediate land. At subsequent dates, probably in the late 1760s, Boulton acquired a number of other parcels of common land on a less secure basis as a tenant-at-will (which in essence meant that he could be given notice to quit at the end of a year). These he enclosed, and they comprised the remainder of the mill pool, the area used for 'the island pool', the 'little pool' and the land adjoining it, and the lower lawn and part of Great Hockley Pool – making a further 12 acres.[2] It was in these 25 acres that his initial landscaping was carried out.

The land lay in an extensive area of unenclosed common, the greater part forming Handsworth Heath, adjoining the smaller surviving common of Birmingham Heath to the west. Hockley Brook, a tributary of the River Tame, formed the boundary between the two parishes, and also at that time between the counties of Staffordshire and Warwickshire. The soil was thin, infertile, hungry and quick draining and supported a heath vegetation of 'gorse, ling and thorn,' but no trees (*see* Plate 2). At the time Ruston had acquired the original lease, much of the land had been the Lord of the Manor's rabbit warren, and the common was used for rough grazing by the freeholders of Handsworth, though Boulton encroached onto this heath, making roads and establishing plantations; he also rented other land in Handsworth as a farm.[3] By 1769 he also leased land to the south adjoining Soho in the parish of Birmingham.[4]

The Soho site had considerable changes of levels and from the highest point at 450 feet (137.15 metres) where the house stood the ground fell sharply some 60 feet (18.29 metres) to the mill, whilst the land in front of the house sloped away more gently. Because of its position, the house commanded good views in all directions. Apart from the Soho mill pool which Ruston and Eaves had constructed, the area had a number of other pools created for industrial use, such as the Great Hockley Pool to the east, made earlier to provide water for Aston furnace. Above this pool on the hillside there was also 'the little pool', fed by a spring and probably formed as a result of gravel extraction. Subsequently Boulton enlarged the little pool and added to the man-made pools by creating 'the island pool' below the Manufactory in 1775, and this was later amalgamated with the adjoining Great Hockley Pool.

Before all other considerations, Boulton's reason for acquiring the site had been the opportunity it gave him to use water-power to create a major industrial development and to allow him to expand his manufacturing business far beyond what his father had been able to achieve in the limited available space in Birmingham town centre. His alterations to the pools, and the cutting of canals, were designed primarily to increase the water available for the Manufactory's water-wheel, but he also regarded the areas of water as features which added greatly to the setting of Soho. Indeed, an American visitor to Soho in 1776 neatly encapsulated this dual aspect of Soho:

> His house is on a fine spot. His gardens are beautiful, interspersed with Canals, which are nothing more than his mill Damb and his Races, [from] which he has ingeniously constructed the *Dulce* as well as the *Utile*. Over these he has bridges, and other good objects, which are not a little beautiful.[5]

It is clear from Boulton's many notes that he saw Soho not only in terms of profit, but also of beauty. The Manufactory, the Mint, Soho House, the pools, the gardens, park, and farm were one entity and a testimony to his creativity and achievement – 'the Monument I have raised to myself'.[6]

In the early years of their marriage, Boulton and his second wife, Ann, whom he had married in 1760, lived at the Boulton family home in Snow Hill, Birmingham. They did not move to Soho House until 1766, but even before this he carried out some landscaping in the vicinity of the newly-finished house, planting 'above 2000 firs' and 'a great variety of shrubs' to give the house protection from the prevailing winds.[7] These were planted in an arc to the south of the house and to the north-east parallel to the line of the former main road. A kitchen garden was also formed on land to the south of the Manufactory. He must also have enclosed the land with posts and rails, created a driveway to the house up the hill from the Manufactory, and made a lawn in front of the house with paddocks beyond. Soho House was initially occupied by his mother, Mrs Christiana Boulton, and one of her daughters, and then from *c*.1763 by Boulton's new business partner, John Fothergill, who had agreed,

> to keep the place in the same good order he found it in but F[othergill] soon distinguish'd that his love for money was greater than for a garden and the whole would soon have become a desert but B[oulton] being unwilling to see what he had taken so much pains about fall to ruin he offered to be at one half of the expense himself and in consequence thereof the garden hath been in some degree preserved but the land (wch F alone was to reap the fruits of) is much impoverished haveing not received the assistance of one L[oa]d of muck since F's residence.[8]

Once Fothergill moved out (much against his will) and Boulton and his wife went to live at Soho in 1766, Boulton was able to exert close control over the maintenance of the gardens and plan and execute further improvements.

Boulton does not appear to have drawn any plans with his ideas for the landscaping of Soho, or if he did, those plans have not been found. Indeed, no maps show the Soho estate prior to 1785, and then only as part of Handsworth Heath, so that the exact chronology of the changes is difficult to establish. Nor did he commit his ideas to paper, with one exception, as he did for the enlarged Soho estate after 1794 (*see* Chapter Two). What is certain is that the development of the gardens was very much Boulton's concept. He was a man who absorbed new ideas very quickly, who observed much and travelled widely and who had an innate sense of design. Many letters survive concerning his planned alterations to the Manufactory, the Mint, the engine yard, and the laying out of the workmen's gardens, leaving no room for doubt that the landscaping of Soho was well within his capabilities. Further evidence of what was done at Soho comes from Boulton's private cash books, a considerable number of nurserymen's bills and detailed workmen's bills.

How much the landscape was Boulton's own work is indicated by a verse in one of his notebooks which he addressed to 'the crityks in Land[ski]p Gard[ening]':

> No Forest, but a Garden neat
> An easy Walk a resting seat
> Made from the barren Wast by me
> Who planted every Flower and Tree
> To skreen me from the NE Broose
> And most of all my self to please
> Nor Knight nor Price nor Burk sublime
> I ape, in Landskip, nor in Rhime.[9]

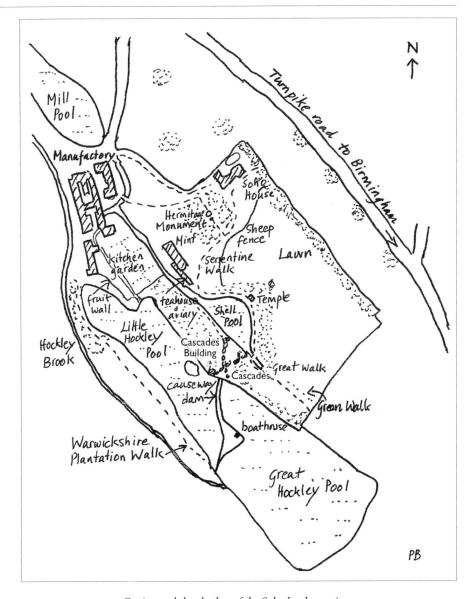

1 *Conjectural sketch plan of the Soho landscape in 1794.*

This is similar to a verse in a poem on Soho 'addressed to Matthew Boulton esq by a friend who saw Soho when Mr B[oulton] first settled there, in 1775, and saw it again in 1796 in its improv'd state',[10] which features the Goddess of Invention who sketches a plan for Soho, realised by Boulton. What he achieved between the early 1760s and 1794 is shown in Fig. 1.

Although Boulton disclaimed the influence of prominent writers in landscaping, such as Knight, Price and Burke, from the early 1770s he was aware of what was being published on the subject. In his diary for 1771 he noted: 'Essay on ornamental gardening supposed to be wrote by Mr Whateley'.[11] This was Thomas Whateley's

Observations on Modern Gardening and Laying out Pleasure Grounds, published in 1770, which included descriptions of 15 gardens and natural scenes with connecting text and provided a lucid account of the theory of English gardening.[12] It is not known whether or not Boulton did purchase Whateley's book and another influential work, which he described as 'Mason's poem on gardening'; the latter appeared under 'Memorandum on what to buy' in his notebook for 1772.[13] William Mason's *The English Garden, a Poem*, published in 1772, expressed admiration for the work of Capability Brown, and gave his view of the Natural style in verse. He also described the flower garden he created for George Harcourt, Viscount Nuneham, at Nuneham Courtenay, Oxfordshire, which included a Temple of Flora,[14] and may have inspired Boulton to create a similar feature at Soho. Boulton certainly possessed a first edition of Sir Williams Chambers' *A Dissertation on Oriental Gardening*, published in 1772, in which Chambers criticised the close copying of nature which prevailed in many English gardens.[15] He also owned James Justice's *The Scot's Gardiners Director*, published in 1754.[16]

In July 1772 Boulton visited Surrey and saw a number of places including Epsom, Cobham and Claremont. However, it was his visit to the nearby estate

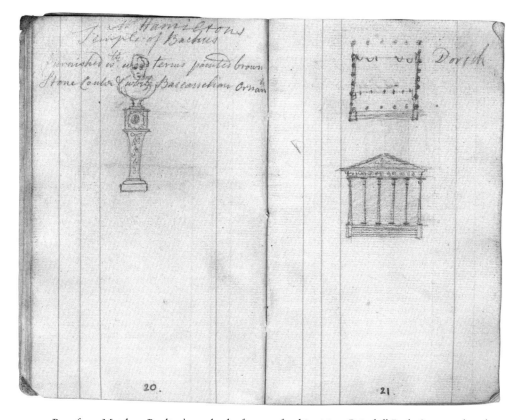

2   *Page from Matthew Boulton's notebook of 1772 after his visit to Painshill Park, Surrey, where he sketched the 'Dorick' Temple and its pedestal with Bacchanalian ornaments.*

of Painshill which most caught his attention and was to be influential in the landscaping of Soho. When Boulton saw Painshill, created by Charles Hamilton from the 1740s onwards, it was already on the market due to mounting debts. The estate of over 300 acres established on sandy soil in heathland was remarkable for the number and variety of its trees, its garden buildings and its lake, with islands, created by damming the River Mole.[17] Boulton's five pages of notes on Painshill include notes on the grotto which he considered 'past discription … there are many winding cells to pray in whilst water fills [and] raises ye Idea of Coolness both to the ear and feel and although tis built above yet it seems to be underground'. He also noted a 'very fine Cedar of Lebanon 25 yrs planted', and 'Mr Hamilton's Temple of Bacchus furnished w[i]th wood terms painted brown stone couler and white Baccanalian ornam'.[18]

Robert Adam had a hand in the decoration of the Temple at Painshill which was finished in 1762. Four years later Boulton met Adam when they discussed silverware designs for the Earl of Shelburne, so it is possible he may have heard about the building then, though it would be some years before he saw it for himself. Boulton's Painshill notes included a plan and elevation of the Temple and a sketch of 'a bust of an Emperor on a pedestal'. The notes are interspersed by an observation headed 'Improve Soho', so clearly the visit immediately triggered a number of ideas. The influence of Painshill on Boulton's thinking may have been that a beautiful landscape could be created in an area of similarly infertile and unpromising soil, and that it was important to have expanses of water, a variety of garden buildings, fine trees and varied walks – all of which he eventually achieved at Soho.

However, other influences were nearer to hand. It is inconceivable that he would not have visited two renowned gardens in the Midlands, both landscaped by their owners – George Lyttelton's Hagley and The Leasowes at Halesowen, created by William Shenstone as a *ferme ornée* from 1743. Indeed, Boulton was on terms of friendship with Shenstone[19] and likewise knew a subsequent owner of The Leasowes. Anne Boulton also stayed there in 1792.[20] William Shenstone had advised John Baskerville when he created his garden at Easy Hill, Birmingham, in the 1750s, and Boulton was a close friend of Baskerville. Boulton may also have seen Sir Samuel Hellier's Woodehouse estate at Wombourne, which took some of its inspiration from the Leasowes and had a notable range of garden buildings on a hillside setting and where visitors were encouraged in the 1760s-70s.[21] Inspiration may also have come from estates owned by industrialists in the Birmingham region where mill pools had a secondary function as ornamental water in landscaped grounds – those of Joseph Webster at Penns, Sutton Coldfield and Samuel Galton at Duddeston in Aston. In addition to these he would have seen the work of Capability Brown, as his Lunar Society friend, the botanist and physician Dr William Withering, resided at Edgbaston Hall, which had been landscaped for a previous occupant by Capability Brown.

As previously noted, the soil at Soho was typical heathland soil: thin and hungry. Matthew Boulton's method for dealing with it must have been developed early on when he initially planted trees and shrubs in the early 1760s, and he used the same method for his subsequent improvements. First it was necessary to remove the existing vegetation, generally by burning it. For example, in June 1772 Boulton paid £1 4s. 4d. to Thomas Keen for 'burning grass and ling in the enclosure'.[22] After this the ground was levelled and trenched, either by double digging or ploughing. It was then spread with different dressings to give it body, starting with marl applied in winter, spread '1 inch thick or 140 loads to an acre';[23] lime was also applied. The land was then spread with dung or muck, some of which came from Boulton's own horses but most of which was purchased from Birmingham, which generated large quantities.[24] Boulton also made a manure by mixing mud from the pools with dung.[25] Manuring was so vital that Boulton was said to value manure more than money.[26] Finally, new soil was spread at the same rate as the marl; in June 1772 Boulton paid £2 9s. 6d. for 'labourers at the fallow spreading 140 load soil'.[27] Great care had to be taken that new plants, particularly trees, were watered until established. Among the items recorded in Boulton's private cash accounts were '2 watering pans' in February 1770, 'new wheels and new tire to water cart' in December 1776, and in April 1779 'the watering machine' – probably a water cart with an integral hand-pump of the type which had been developed in the 17th century. Subsequently Boulton applied technology to the problem and devised new methods including 'the flooding machine'.

With the soil thus enriched, the years immediately following Boulton's visit to Painshill in 1772 saw a concentration on erecting a variety of garden buildings and features and laying out walks. In his Painshill notes under the heading 'Improve Soho' he had written, 'A Bridg opposite Egginton's for company to walk the round and so that a one horse chair may go round and go over the little pool and a mow'd walk along the brow of the hill Plant at bottom by side the Great Pool low trees'.[28]

The evidence would suggest that even before visiting Painshill, Boulton had embarked on one garden building, a grotto, although its location is uncertain and it may have been a rectangular building at the northern edge of the plantation around what became Shell Pool. In August 1769 William Envill of Bath wrote to Boulton that he had sent fossils and curious stones costing £4 18s. 6d., for his grotto and that he could get more.[29] Bisset's poem on Soho included the line 'verdant lawns, cool grots and peaceful bow'rs', so there may have been more than one grotto. In Matthew Robinson Boulton's accounts for 1833 there is the entry '90 hooks for Groto house',[30] so it was a building which was valued and kept in repair.

A Serpentine Walk led from the house to the 'little pool' on the hillside, the topography dictating the form it took and the name it was given. This little pool was the focus of much activity. The first improvement was the construction of a

cascade or waterfall from the pool down the slope to Great
Hockley Pool in 1774, John Smallwood having been paid £2
15s. 8d. for 'drawing stones to cascade' in December 1773.[31]
The cascade was probably installed as an ornamental feature
but with the practical purpose of acting as a storm water
drain, much damage having occurred from flooding the
previous autumn. A second cascade with a series of small
pools was built in 1775-6, transecting the first cascade and
flowing into the newly created lower pool. It was constructed
of 96 tons of 'Rowley Rags' (a local stone), and in the autumn
of 1776 'leather for the little pool cascade' was paid for,
presumably for pipes to convey the water from pool to pool.[32]
The cascades were enclosed with green-painted palisades to
stop grazing animals straying on to them. A poem on Soho
described the effect of the cascades:

> *Down the hill,*
> *Dashes, with Alpine Grace, the glitt'ring rill*[33]

An American visitor in May 1777, Samuel Curwen,
commented on what was clearly a work in progress:

> Walkt out to Soho, so called being Bolton and Forthergill's
> [*sic*] manufactory house and works and gardens, the nature
> of the ground capable of improvement in an high degree, they already consist of
> gravel walks in the serpentine form, shrubbery, flower borders, ponds of water, an
> occasional cascade &c, &c, running down a narrow pebbled oval over a slope some
> length and emptying itself in a pond below making 2 artificial ponds.[34]

In 1776 Matthew Boulton's private cash book included payments for bricks,
timber and lime for 'a cascade building', also described as a 'cascade library room'
in the accounts.[35] This may be the tower-like brick building evident on the left of
a sketch of the cascade by John Phillp, which is reminiscent of Painshill's Gothic
Tower. After Boulton had a library in his extended house this building was pulled
down in 1801.[36]

The same sketch also gives a glimpse of the temple on the hillside above the
'little pool'. In the winter of 1775-6 there were many payments for levelling the
ground, making paths, and moving stone in preparation, and in October 1776
Benjamin Wyatt was paid £43 10s. 7d. for building it. There was a separate
payment to William Bromley for constructing 51 steps up to it. A payment for 24
tons of limestone in June 1777 may have been for this building.[37] The design of the
temple was clearly inspired by Hamilton's Temple of Bacchus at Painshill, which

3 *Pencil sketch by John Phillp of the cascade from Shell Pool to Little Hockley Pool with the 'cascade library room' on the left, c.1794.*

Boulton had seen in 1772 and sketched in his notebook. Boulton's temple was likewise of 'Dorick' columns (*see* Fig. 30, p.53), though only four of them. However, in Boulton's collection of architectural drawings there is an undated sketch for a temple with six Doric columns.[38] This may be an alternative design for the Temple of Flora, as it was subsequently called, or for another temple Boulton was planning in 1795.[39] John Phillp's watercolour (*see* Plate 3) shows the Temple of Flora with green-painted shutters to protect the interior from the elements. The floor was of quarry tiles and the temple was extensively repaired in 1795.[40]

In April 1778 the 'little pool' was embellished by a large artificial shell installed where the spring water ran into the top of the pool (*see* Fig. 4), and this together with alterations to its shape led to its being called Shell Pool from then on (the pool in the grotto at Painshill also has a large artificial shell feature though it is not known when it was installed). A plan of this area sketched by Boulton, in fact the only surviving plan in Boulton's hand of a specific area of the garden, made in 1790, shows the walk round the pool and two tubs. Perhaps the little tub was 'the large

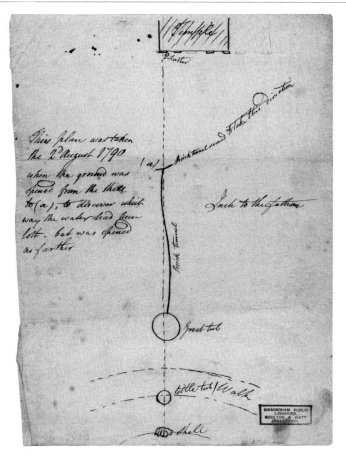

4 *Matthew Boulton's 1790 plan of the area between the Temple of Flora and Shell Pool.*

china jar that stands in the garden' which cost the large sum of £5 in 1770,[41] whilst the great tub was probably made of wood and was referred to as 'Diogene's tub' when it was repaired in 1795.[42] The creation of a flower garden and the extensive planting of trees and shrubs around the temple and its pool took place in 1787-8. A glimpse of Matthew Boulton enjoying the pool is given in a letter to his son in 1788 – 'since your departure we have applied the 4 inch little brass steam engine to the boat in my little pool and it drives it about merrily. I intend to put it upon the Birmingham Canal, in order to see the possibility of sailing up rivers against the stream or sailing without sails against winds and tydes.'[43]

 The 'little pool' was above an area of water created in 1775. This 'lower pool and island', as it was termed, was made from land below the Manufactory. The creation of this new pool was in order to trap water to be returned to the water-wheel in the Manufactory. Boulton himself paid for half the work from his own account[44] and he took 'the new land', which was a peninsula below the Manufactory and an island. The peninsula became a part of the kitchen garden and the island, planted with trees and intended for swans, is shown in one of Phillp's sketches (*see* Plate 4). The pool was extended several times and eventually was amalgamated with Great

Hockley Pool in the 1820s. Boulton was especially fond of what he had created in this area of the garden, even after the second Mrs Boulton was found dead in the little pool in 1783, having apparently fallen in as a result of some kind of stroke or fit.[45]

Other garden buildings at Soho erected in the 1770s included boathouses, one of which was built on a peninsula on the causeway dam separating the two pools. Visitors to Soho might be taken for a sail in M.R. Boulton's boat, though the experience was not for the faint-hearted as Patty Fothergill described in August 1793, when her sister 'was in such a terrible fright when we put up the Sails we were oblig'd to make to the shore as fast as possible' but she and another guest 'staid till a very heavy shower of rain drove us in.'[46]

There was also an observatory. It was octagonal and built of brick but its location is undocumented. In 1768 Boulton had thought of 'a round building for my study, Library etc' and in 1772 when considering an observatory wrote, 'Qr if I could not have a circular top out of my house'.[47] He finally decided on a separate building; work started on it in March 1774 and the equipment was installed the following year.[48] The astronomer Alexander Aubert, visiting Soho in 1778, wrote,'When I was at Soho I had a sight of a little round building in which I observed a Telescope of large aperture, and could not but lament it's having suffered much by rain and weather which the roof did not shelter it from'.[49] Not surprisingly, there were already many entries in Matthew Boulton's private cash book for repairs to the telescope between December 1776 and August 1777, and

5 *An octagonal building, probably the observatory, by John Phillp, 1796.*

Aubert subsequently bought the instrument for £20. There is an illustration in the Phillp Album of an eight-sided brick building with a central aperture, which could be the observatory. It is also possible that it is a pump house, for it is shown with smoke or steam coming from the roof. Repairs to a pump house were carried out in 1778, but its location, like that of the observatory, is undocumented. After 1799 the observatory in the garden was superseded by the observatory platform on the roof of the remodelled house, complete with a new telescope.

From 1775 onwards Boulton also developed a part of the garden near Soho House. In a grove of trees dating from his initial plantings in the early 1760s he erected a stone monument in memory of his friend and member of the Lunar Society, Dr William Small, soon after the latter's death in February 1775. Writing to James Watt some time later he said:

> Messrs Keir, Darwin, Day and self have never yet agreed about a monument for the Church, but as there is nothing which I wish to fix in my mind so permanently as the remembrance of my dear departed friend, I did not delay to erect one to his memory in the prettiest but most obscure part of my garden; a part that is modelled, at least characterised, since you were here. 'Tis a sepulchred grove, in which is a building adapted for contemplation; from one of its windows, under a Gothic arch framed by trees, you see the church in which he was interred [St Philip's] and no other object whatsoever except the monument. It is a sarcophagus standing upon a pedestal.[50]

On the sarcophagus were verses in memory of Dr Small written by Erasmus Darwin, which included the lines:

> If chance ye enter these sequestere'd groves,
> And day's bright sunshine for a while forego,
> O leave to Folly's cheek the laughs and loves,
> And give one hour to philosophic woe![51]

This bears a strong resemblance to Shenstone's groves at the Leasowes which had verses on monuments in memory of dead friends. The 'building adapted for contemplation', started in 1776 at the same time as the urn was erected, was probably the round building with gothic windows illustrated by John Phillp (see frontispiece and Plate 5). Its walls were of bark and it had a thatched roof. Again, it bears some resemblance to the hermitage at Painshill. The rough exterior, however, had a sophisticated interior with a wooden floor and plastered walls; a panelled door painted pale blue whilst the frame and skirting board were pink (see Plate 6). Between the glazed windows there was a plaster or wood medallion portrait of an unidentified man thought to be possibly Matthew Boulton, with attributes connected with gardening and farming; this may have been based on a French book of architectural ornaments, Recueil Contenant Frises d'ornements, by G. Huquier, which Boulton owned.[52] This building is probably the one referred to in Boulton's private account book as the Hermitage in 1778-9, when there were several payments to a carpenter, including for 'glueing ornaments'. It was repaired in 1793 with further payments for carpenter's work.[53]

Another garden building was the tea room with a menagerie, built in 1776-9. The menagerie, built first, was a long, narrow, slightly curved structure which overlooked the canal leading from Shell Pool to the Manufactory. In 1777 work started on the tea room which ran east-west and which abutted the menagerie. The exact design of these structures is not clear as there is no illustration of them, and no plan until 1788. However, it would appear from the payments to workmen that the menagerie had roughcast walls and a tiled roof, together with a large amount of timber work, presumably for the pens. William Hutton, the Birmingham paper dealer, supplied 'paper for covering the menagrie' in May 1777 and John Ryland, Birmingham's first wire drawer, supplied six straight wires for it in October. Brick steps were added in April 1778. An area within the menagerie was described

6 *Monument erected by Matthew Boulton on the death of his friend and fellow Lunar Society member Dr William Small in 1775. The monument could be viewed from the 'building adapted for contemplation', i.e. the Hermitage, and is illustrated in J.P. Muirhead's* The Life of James Watt *(1858).*

as a kitchen and this had plastered walls and a fireplace. The menagerie was, as was usual at the time, really an aviary and there are no payments for animals, other than farm animals or domestic pets (including a monkey), but there were payments in 1778 for birds such as a macaw and a pea hen, together with white turkeys, geese, chickens and ducks. In October 1779 John Smith supplied 'pullies for bird cages.'[54]

The tea room was a more substantial single-storey structure of three interconnecting rooms and had a fireplace supplied and fitted by a local architect, William Hollins, who often did work for Boulton. It may also have had an elaborate decorative scheme, as Henry Bird was paid six guineas when it was first painted in 1779.[55] In 1781-2 Matthew Boulton equipped two of the rooms at the tea room

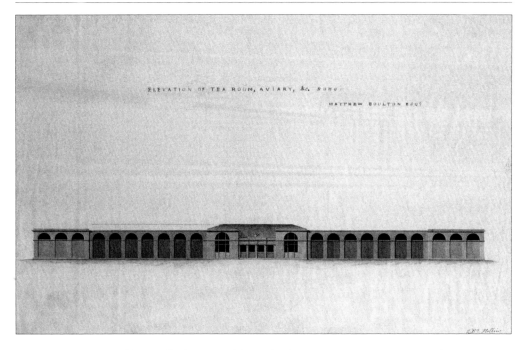

ELEVATION OF TEA ROOM, AVIARY, &c. SOHO.

MATTHEW BOULTON ESQ

7   *William Hollins's proposed design for the tea room and aviary, 1797. The tea room,*
with the aviary (sometimes referred to as the menagerie) as a wing on the right, was
built in 1776-9 to entertain the increasing number of visitors calling to view the Soho
Manufactory. Hollins's proposal to add a wing on the left was probably never carried
out, and the tea room subsequently became the entrance to the Mint.

for more specialised use, one becoming a fossil room and the other a laboratory.
Among the items ordered for the fossil room were 700 square china pans supplied
by Wedgwood in May 1785.[56] Boulton was much interested in fossils and had
been buying them for some time. In his diary for May 1769 he had noted 'John
Birch of Castleton I bought some fossels of and he says he will get some more'.[57]
A ground plan of the tea room dating to the Spring of 1788[58] shows the three
interconnecting rooms which measured altogether 43½ feet (13.26 metres) long.
By this date Matthew Boulton had established in his private garden an industrial
building which was the world's first steam-powered mint. This plan shows only
one doorway which leads into the central tea room, but it does not include the
fenestration. Another plan of c.1795,[59] which does include the fenestration, shows
that all three rooms had windows right along the walls looking on to the canal and
the pool below.

William Hollins had a subsequent association with the tea room and aviary when
he prepared a new design for it in March 1797.[60] This was probably a modification
to the existing structure. To give a sense of symmetry he proposed another aviary
to the west of what would then become a central tea room. It is probable that he
also designed alterations to the windows of the laboratory and tea room, which

were reduced in width and arched to fit in with the arches of the menagerie (aviary) pens. The three blanked-off arched areas could have been the menagerie kitchen. However, the second aviary was never built, the space being used instead for the new coining room of 1798-9. Nevertheless, in 1798-9 Benjamin Wyatt carried out some alterations to the 'elaboratory and scullery' which may have been to Hollins's design,[61] and in 1799 the menagerie walls were repaired.

The tea room was used on an occasion in 1788, for entertaining distinguished visitors to Soho, as Boulton wrote to his son, who was then continuing his education in Germany:

> I have been fatigued with much comp[an]y at Soho lately amongst others were the Duke and Duchess of Northumberland with some of their relations and after fatiguing them in the manufactory I took them to the Tea Room where I had provided the best fruits, cakes, Biskets, sweetmeats and wine to refresh them.[62]

It was also used as an entrance point to the Mint for distinguished visitors and was sometimes a convenient place for taking meals: in 1804 Boulton, engaged on filling an order for coinage, wrote to James Watt, 'We dine in the Tea Room and do not quit the work till nine when all is locked up and our military guard on duty'.[63]

The buildings were only one aspect of the improvements to the grounds and much work was done in making walks and building ornamental bridges where the paths crossed water courses. A walk was also made in the western Warwickshire plantation, which Boulton started planting two years after leasing the land from Lord Archer, the Lord of the Manor of Birmingham, in 1775, partly as the site for the new pool. John Snape's *Plan of the Parish of Birmingham* surveyed in 1779 clearly shows a thin belt of planting along the length of the new pool on the Birmingham side. Boulton also carried out planting on Handsworth Common in 1788,[64] establishing clumps of trees in the land between the old line of the main road and the turnpike road of 1725-7. Work was also carried out on landscaping around Soho House. A wall was built at the back of the house to give privacy from the foot road to the Manufactory which passed close by, and an oval lawn with a small pool was laid out. The front of the house had a large gravel sweep and then lawn with a white-painted net and chain sheep fence across it to prevent animals straying up to the house (*see* Fig. 20, p.34).[65]

The creation of the gardens at Soho involved planting on an exceptional scale considering their size, but none of the natural vegetation was 'garden worthy' and there were no field trees on the site that could be retained to give a feeling of maturity. A considerable body of evidence survives for the planting at Soho from itemised nurserymen's bills, though the accounts indicate that these form a fraction of what was actually purchased. Between February 1768 and November 1779 Matthew Boulton paid 17 nurserymen's bills,[66] most of which covered several orders in one bill. He purchased his plants from nurserymen up to 30 miles away, though seeds were sometimes ordered from London suppliers. No evidence survives of the supplier of the '2000 firs and a quantity of shrubs' in the early 1760s, but once Boulton lived at Soho he purchased almost exclusively for 10 years from a Coventry nurseryman, John Whittingham. However, the earliest surviving bill was from James Bramall of Lichfield who supplied Boulton with 'six thousand quicksetts' [hawthorn] at 6s. a thousand,[67] which were probably planted as hedging in conjunction with new post and rail fencing. In the 1770s Boulton switched to the firm of Brunton and Forbes, who had a nursery at Quinton, but he sublet them some land near Hockley as additional nursery ground. He also had an area set out as a nursery ground near Shell Pool.

The trees listed in surviving bills (*see* for example, Fig. 8) are predominantly conifers, though the evidence of John Phillp's sketches in the late 1790s, when the plantings would have been from 20 to 30 years old, shows that deciduous species were also used. The initial '2000 firs' could have been the silver fir (*Abies alba*) or the Norway spruce, then called spruce fir (*Picea abies*), or the balm of Gilead fir (*Abies balsamea*), all of which were also planted at Soho in the 1770s and 1780s. Other conifers were 'American spruce', either *Picea glauca* or *Picea mariana*, Weymouth pine (*Pinus strobus*), 'Scotch firs', now Scots pine (*Pinus sylvestris*), and white cedars (*Thuja occidentalis*). Larches were also used, sometimes as specimen trees. Deciduous trees specified in bills were planes (*Platanus x hispanica*), weeping willows (*Salix babylonica*) used on the island, and birches (*Betula pendula*). A bill from Brunton and Forbes in 1788 for '15 Weymouth Pine 4 ft, 200 Scotch Firs 2 ft, and 20 Spruce 2ft'[68] may have been for the tree clumps on Handsworth Common planted in that year.

The major evidence for shrubs at Soho comes from two consignments of plants from Brunton and Forbes in 1787 and 1788 for planting on either side of the Temple of Flora; the latter consignment included '200 evergreen and flowering shrubs' and '300 fine Herbaceous plants'.[69] Boulton was particularly fond of flowering plants, an interest he encouraged in his daughter, Anne, who first learnt botany with William Withering. Dr Withering and his wife were staying at Soho House in the summer of 1784 while their house in Edgbaston was being repainted and it was where Withering worked on his book *An Account of the Foxglove*. Anne was recovering from whooping cough and her father was in Cornwall. Boulton wrote to his 16-year-old daughter,

> when I consider that Dr Withering is observing your constitution & teaching you Botany I am quite reconcild to the Fates that brought you to Soho so soon, not doubting but you will endeavour to avail your self of so favourable an opportunity.... Moreover I should rejoyce much if you would but qualify your self to teach me Botany at my return & then we will have a Botanical Garden.[70]

However, Anne's love of flowers had been acknowledged at an earlier age, for a portrait of her as a young girl, painted probably by Tilly Kettle in c.1778, shows

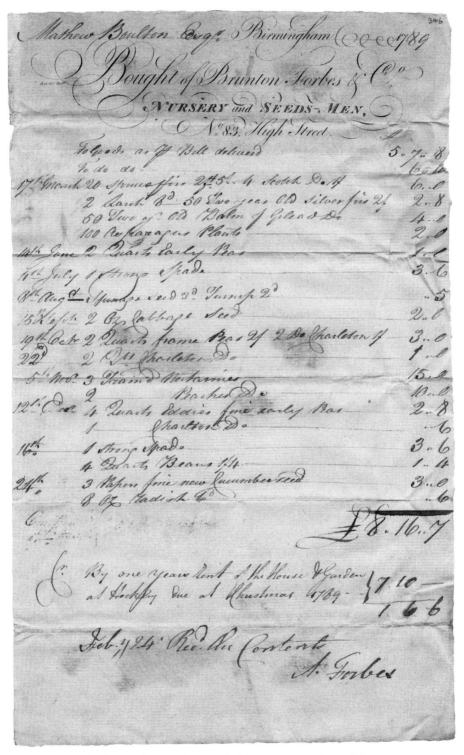

8 *Plant order for Matthew Boulton supplied by Brunton, Forbes and Co. in 1789.*

her with an apron full of annual and perennial flowers which she is arranging in a flower stand.[71] The nurserymen were evidently aware of Anne's interest in botany and gardens, as a letter from James Hunter about the shrubs and flowering plants sent in April 1788 for the Temple of Flora, notes in the general instructions about the planting:

> The Plants and Shrubs, according to the inclos'd list, are this Day forwarded to the Soho where we hope they will arrive safe and please.
>
> Please to order all the Shrubs No. 3 [the tallest] to be Planted in the back part of the shrubry, each side the Temple of Flora and as many of the Others as can conveniently be put in, as the Plantation is at Pres[en]t much too thin, of both Shrubs and Herbaceous Plants –
>
> If the plants now sent, are well varied and mixd, they will add much to the beauty of the Plant[atio]n, as well as furnish Miss Boulton with a great variety of choice flowers for her amusement in the Botanical system
>
> Should there be any Plants left of the 1st and 2d Class after the above plantation is compleated, they may be Planted along the border on the other side of the Pool Mr Boulton will please to order the gardener [to] turn up the Turf, for about half a yd round where [each] of the rhododendrons are to be Planted and as the soil in that place is not of the black peaty kind the pres[en]t should be taken out and the hole filld up with some of the same sort as the border consists of on the other side of the Pool – but these Rhododendrons may be kep'd in some Sheltered situation till the beginning of May, before they are turned out the pots, but not to be put in the Hot House or any very warm situation[72]

The two rhododendrons were *Rhododendron maximum*, introduced from North America in the 1730s, which cost 9s., and *Rhododendron ponticum*, more recently introduced from Asia Minor in the 1760s, which cost 7s. 6d. These were expensive novelties when compared to the £3 15s. paid for the 300 shrubs and the £2 10s. for the 200 herbaceous plants.

Of the 200 'evergreen and flowering shrubs' in the order, those sent to give height to the back of the border included maples, acacias, stagshorn sumachs and viburnums, whilst the medium height shrubs included jasmines, Persian lilacs, brooms, berberis, hypericums and hydrangeas; the lowest shrubs included honeysuckles (then grown along the ground), roses, Jerusalem sage, periwinkles, daphnes and box. These were mixed with 300 'fine herbaceous plants' some of them English natives and others introductions from Europe and North America. These were likewise graded as to height, the tallest including golden rod, white rosebay willow herb, phloxes, alkanet and loosestrife, the middle range including yellow foxglove, sneezewort, red valerian and bellflowers and the lowest including yellow fumitory, sweet Williams, cranesbills and many double forms of English native plants such as wood anemones, celandines and lady's smock.

A flower garden was established in the area of the hovel or hermitage and perhaps an earlier order from Brunton and Forbes in 1783 for 304 herbaceous plants and 18 pinks and carnations had been for this location.[73] Flowering plants were also grown in beds in the lawn in front of the house. These beds probably included annuals for which there are no detailed lists, the seedsmen's bills simply recording 'sundry flower seeds', '30 sorts hardy annuals' or '40 papers flower seeds', although mignonette seeds were listed in one bill. Boulton was, however, very fond of marigolds and perhaps had been introduced to this plant by John Baskerville who had passed on to him the list of plants he had ordered from James Gordon of Fenchurch Street, London, in November 1766; this included African marigolds, iris, sweet peas, morning glory, double nasturtiums, Jerusalem cross and sweet sultans, together with double Dutch jonquils and Van Thol tulips.[74] Bulbs featured in some of the bills for Soho, and as well as being planted in the borders were also forced for the house – the inventory of ormolu stock in 1782 included '2 bulbous root pots, in Mr Boulton's house'.[75]

The gardens of Soho House were not only ornamental but also productive, and shortly after acquiring the Soho lease Boulton laid out a kitchen garden. When he came to live at Soho he rented additional land as a small hobby farm.

The kitchen garden was on a site south-east of the Manufactory and it was partly enclosed by walls, the first fruit wall being built in 1774; a new fruit wall was built in 1776 on the promontory of land left between the tail race and the main channel of the Hockley Brook as part of the creation of the new pool the previous year (see Plate 4).[76] The area of the fruit walls and the kitchen garden were very susceptible to flooding, the worst flood occurring in 1785 when John Ford of Hockley Abbey raised the level of the dam of Great Hockley Pool.[77] Alterations were carried out several times in attempts to remedy the problem, building up the walls and raising the level of land. Ten years later Boulton decided to 'mud the upper pool, when the island pool is muddied pump up the water first into mill pool and make a dam at bottom of kitchen garden'.[78]

The layout of Boulton's kitchen garden was the standard 18th-century arrangement of four plots divided by gravel walks, and the beds may have been edged by dwarf box.[79] It was usual to practise rotation in a kitchen garden, having one part grass for use as a drying green, and this appears to have been done at Soho for William Cheshire's report in May 1797 of the workers in the garden included two mowing in the kitchen garden.[80]

The wide range of vegetables grown at Soho can be discussed with reference to surviving bills for vegetable seeds. As an example, the seeds supplied by Minire and Mason in 1772 included two varieties of onions, leeks, two of carrots, parsnip, salsify, three of turnip, five of radish, two of beet, two of endive, three of celery, seven of cabbage, two of kale, cauliflower, five of broccoli, nine of beans, five of peas, two of spinach, two of melon, five of salad cucumber, two of lettuce, two of mustard and cress, three of parsley, marjoram and chervil.[81] The multiple varieties would have provided successive cropping. From other bills the following were also grown: early potatoes, sea kale, salsify, scorzonera, gourds, asparagus, garlic, marrows, fennel, rhubarb and Brussels sprouts. Most of the orders for vegetable seeds included several pounds of hops for use in brewing beer for the household. For raising early crops and for growing cucumbers and melons there were frames and hot beds. The hot beds were wooden-framed, filled with dung and covered with glazed lights. These were probably not within the kitchen garden but near the dung yard associated with the stables. In 1801 Boulton decided to 'widen the gravil walk by the melon ground so my chair will pass'.[82] Hot beds had been in use at Soho before 1770, as in March 1770 William Farnol, glass merchant of 20 Upper Priory, Birmingham, was paid 6s. 4d. for mending hot bed glass, and the next month paid £1 4s. 8d. for glazing two new frames for hot beds.[83] A surviving bill from him from 24 October 1771 to 29 April 1772 included glass for the house, stable doors, hot house, hot bed lights and garden lights.[84] The latter were small rigid cloches. The frames and lights were covered with mats in cold weather and the mats needed to be replaced frequently. Most of the bills for plants and seeds included mats and this, together with the brittleness of the glass and the expense of the dung, made hot beds something of a luxury. It is not clear whether luxury fruits, such as pineapples and grapes, were grown at Soho although Matthew Boulton had a hot house by 1773,[85] and an arrangement made in 1775 with a gardener responsible for the kitchen garden also included raising the produce of the hot house. A page in Boulton's notebook for 1776-8 listed minimum temperatures for a number of plants including pineapples, oranges, myrtle, aloe, Indian fig and several cacti, so perhaps these were grown at Soho.[86] Another specimen plant brought in was a coffee tree, which would have been grown in the hot house as a novelty rather than with any expectation of producing useable berries. It was supplied, along with a pepper plant, some plant pots and a load of tanner's bark (used for hot beds) in 1788.[87] The standard 18th-century hot house was a lean-to erected against a wall but there is no evidence as to whether this was the type Boulton had, or indeed its exact location. The outdoor fruit raised on the fruit wall included peaches, nectarines, 'May Duke' cherries, apricots and plums.

Matthew Boulton's farming activities were certainly in operation by 1768 and he supplemented his Soho land by leasing other parcels. He paid 14 guineas a year to rent the Upper Breaches from the Rev. Mr Birch, which was probably glebe land beyond the Commons on the north side of the Soho turnpike, and could have been from 30 to 50 acres in exent.[88] He acquired further land in 1769 when he started renting meadows from Henry Carver at 10 guineas a year. This was probably about six acres of old enclosures on Birmingham Heath near Winson Green.[89] From 1780 he rented Hockley Brook Farm which lay south-east of Soho, adjoining the boundary with Aston, and at that time probably ceased renting the Upper Breaches. The Soho part of the farm was used for grazing stock in the areas not laid out as plantations, shrubberies or lawns. Several cows were purchased in 1768, paid for by Mrs Boulton.[90] A new cow barn was erected in 1770 and another barn in 1775, both built of wood, and these together with the rickyard were probably near the kitchen garden and either side of the canal from Shell Pool, including the area later used for the Mint. Carver's meadows were used for the production of hay, as was some of the land in the Upper Breaches. However, Boulton expended considerable money and effort in improving this land and his cash book recorded numerous payments for muck and new soil, for squitching and gathering stones and for hedging and ditching. On the land he enclosed he grew turnips and barley as winter food for his stock. He also purchased equipment, such as a plough and a cart. Part of this land was let to the Soho workmen as guinea gardens where they could cultivate vegetables and flowers for their own use.[91]

The size of the labour force employed by Matthew Boulton for the gardens and farm varied greatly, not only seasonally but according to whether major alterations were on hand. Some of the labour for the 'improvements' was provided by men who were principally employed as carpenters, stone-masons and general handymen at the Manufactory and were paid by Boulton himself on day rates for working for him. As an example, between 16 November 1776 and 13 September 1777 William Carless, a carpenter, was employed by Boulton for 101 days working on the menagerie, hanging gates, making a cowshed and constructing bridges.[92] Other people were employed on piece-work, particularly for trenching, ploughing, moving soil, laying drains and work connected with the pools. For example on 4 April 1779, Withers and Bell were paid 'for digging the Warwickshire plantation say 37 roods at 7d a rood 21/7, clearing the walk 4/- and other work 3 day 6/-'.[93] However, the day-to-day work of the garden and farm was usually done by gardeners who employed general labourers on day work. Bills which survive from 1768 show that the one gardener, William Bromley, was employing five labourers working under his supervision, on both garden and farm.[94] However, in the mid-1770s, Boulton employed three men on annual agreements with specific responsibilities. Only the agreement made with Francis Edwards survives but it indicates the range of gardening duties expected of him:

> I hereby promise and agree to give Francis Edwards five pounds per annum and a reasonable quantity of manure for my kitchen garden say not more than I make with my own Horses and Pigs – In consideration of which he shall keep my kitchen garden in clean decent order and furnish my family with all kinds of herbs roots pulse etc etc in as plentiful a manner as it has been hitherto been furnished and all that my family may not have occasion for I will give him liberty to sell in the best manner he can.
>
> I also promise to give him three pounds per annum more in consideration of which he shall give proper attendance to the hot house and hot beds and to give me the produce of the hot house and whatever I may have occasion for, from the hot beds he shall likewise dig, weed, raise and transplant all that may be necessary in the Nursery below the Little pool he shall also gather the fruit Roots herbs pulse etc when wanted but not to have any trouble with pruning trees.

I will further give him Ten pounds per annum more and Henry's help to mow on the mowing mornings. In consideration of which he shall mow all the lawns Dig all the shrubberys once in the front Save all the seeds weed hoe and preserve the flowers NB he may save all the seeds he can but must buy whatever seeds are wanting.[95]

A further note read 'for the year 1776-7 M[atthew] B[oulton] agreed to give him £25 and find him tools and a Bed down at the Cow barn'.[96] The other gardener, Francis Davidson, was paid 14 guineas, whilst Henry was paid 15 guineas; their duties were not recorded, but the plantations, walks and farm would have been their responsibilities and for this they must have been able to hire additional labour.

Whether the other gardeners were given accommodation is unclear, but there are mentions of a gardener's room at the coach house and furniture was purchased for a gardener in December 1788.[97] At this point a new gardener was engaged who was paid 27 guineas per annum.

Whilst the costs of maintaining the Soho gardens by the 1780s were not inconsiderable, these were to be eclipsed by the costs of obtaining the freehold of Soho and creating a setting in a landscape park, which Matthew Boulton achieved in the last 14 years of his life and which is discussed in the next chapter.

Two

A Scene of Picturesque Beauty:
The Enlarged Landscape of Soho, 1794-1809

Phillada Ballard

T he landscaping of Soho was the work of many years, much expense and considerable persistence on Matthew Boulton's part. For nearly 30 years his efforts were confined to a relatively small area, but after purchasing the freehold of Soho in 1794, together with additional land, he was able to work on a wider canvas. That year had seen him turning over in his mind whether or not it would now be prudent to buy the land outright. Characteristically, he made a list of the pros and cons of such a step, as a result of which he concluded that buying the freehold would protect his pleasant views and beloved gardens from development for the near future and his descendants' inheritance in the longer term.[1]

Thus convinced, in November 1794 and again in August 1795, Boulton made purchases of land from George Birch, Lord of the Manor of Handsworth. The first parcel comprised 74 acres and included the original Soho lease and the land held as a tenant-at-will, together with contiguous land to the north-west and south-east of Soho. The second parcel of 12 acres was a long strip of land adjoining the turnpike road beyond Thornhill House. Matthew Boulton took a long-term view of the Soho estate and realised that it had enormous potential value as building land. Of his second purchase from Birch he noted, 'Plan all the land of my last purchase so as to Build many Houses next to the turnpike and as many to face Winson Green,'[2] having had in mind a project to let land for Birmingham people to build 'a small Town upon which from the nature of its situation is to be calld Comfort'.[3] He also was aware that he could let land for building along the turnpike near his own house for profit, 'if I choose to sacrifice my own house by letting off the land by the side of the g[rea]t Road'.[4] However, having negotiated so hard to get this land and bring his holdings up to the turnpike road, in the event he did not sacrifice his privacy.

This was the conclusion of seven years of difficulties with Birch over the Soho land, caused in part by Boulton enclosing and improving land for which he had paid Birch no rent. Boulton had been the initiator of the Handsworth Enclosure Bill which started in 1789 and concluded in 1792; this had awarded land to individual owners in lieu of freeholders' rights, paving the way for unencumbered purchase, and Boulton had subsequently made his first land purchases in Handsworth from Henry Whateley when he acquired Moneybags Farm in 1793. But the Enclosure Bill did not overcome Boulton's problems with Birch, who was reluctant to sell him as much land as he required; Birch, having previously in September 1791 given him notice to quit the Soho land which he held as tenant-at-will, again gave him notice to quit in September 1794.[5] Boulton had contemplated continuing his business at Soho on the land he held by lease, but abandoning his residence and the garden he had laboured so hard on. He considered three other residences in turn – Edgbaston Hall, where he could have taken over William Withering's lease,[6] Aston Hall,[7] and finally the house built by Henry Whateley's father at Handsworth.[8]

Boulton was reluctant to purchase the Soho land unless he could acquire it in sufficient quantities to control the views from his house and prevent others building too close to him. However, Birch wanted a very high price per acre for what was improved land, albeit that it was Boulton who had borne the entire cost of making it so, and was also insisting on more than Boulton wanted to give for the unimproved land because the rapid growth of Birmingham was pushing up land prices in the vicinity. Boulton was also reluctant to acquire the land for a term of years by lease, rather than purchasing the freehold. As Boulton wrote to James Watt in May 1794,

> Shall I who have given the present value to the land and have cultivated it for thirty years past be driven from it, without I conform to terms that Reason and Calculation forbid ... I therefore [choose] not to purchase any or to purchase so much as will secure me from all apprehensions of disputes, and lawsuits about Roads, dams, watercourses etc etc ... When it is considered how large a property I have growing to the freehold, that the beauty of my situation and garden would have been destroyed, and all that money I have layed on all, I am laying out, and all I may lay out, glideing upon the wings of time.[9]

In 'Considerations on buying Soho' he wrote in slightly different terms as to why he wanted the land:

> If I do Buy Soho, the consequences will be, that I shall thereby derive a Controling power over all around me so as to prevent any Buildings from being erected in any place and in any manner that may tend to incommode me, or rob me of any of the natural pleasures of the place... I shall enjoy the fruits of my own labour; Repose myself under my own vine, and my own fig tree ... I shall look back with more satisfaction on the days that are past, and forward with the hopes of my Descendants being opulent and respectable Manufacturers, at Soho, to the third and fourth generation, rather than dependant courtiers.[10]

Boulton was able to extend his controlling power still further after the enclosure of Birmingham Heath in 1798, when in the following year he purchased land he had formerly leased on the Warwickshire side and on which he had made improvements, together with further land giving him control over the margins of the whole of Great Hockley Pool. In all, between 1793 and 1808 he made 26 separate acquisitions of land in Handsworth and Birmingham, mainly by purchase but some by exchange, working towards achieving a unified holding within a single unbroken boundary. This resulted in Boulton owning a long rectangular estate one and a quarter miles long and between a quarter and half a mile wide at different points, altogether in the region of 200 acres. Of this, Soho demesne and homestead, as the land which he had in hand was termed, was 80 acres, and consisted of Boulton's house, pleasure gardens, plantations and farm.

In 1795, therefore, Matthew Boulton, then aged 67, embarked on a programme of improvements which might have daunted a much younger man. As well as remodelling his house, he landscaped the extended grounds of Soho House, and also improved the land of the outlying portions which were let as farms. His ideas of what he wanted to implement are contained in three notebooks which cover the period from October 1795 until April 1803 and contain ad hoc observations on the gardens, lists of trees to be planted, points he wanted the gardener to attend to, queries for Wyatt and miscellaneous thoughts on improvements.[11] No plans of proposed alterations have come to light, with the exception of projected extensions to the walks at Soho, which were pencilled onto a map of his 1793 land holdings in Handsworth (*see* Plate 7).[12] However other evidence is contained in letters, bills from nurserymen and others, in maps of Soho and from Matthew Boulton's financial accounts.

The changes to the layout of the Soho gardens can be seen by comparing the conjectural map of 1795 with the conjectural map of 1809 (*see* Fig. 9). What Matthew Boulton had done was to place his re-modelled house in the setting of a landscaped park, using some of the newly acquired Handsworth land for deep plantations that concealed the roads, such as the turnpike road or the road down to the Manufactory, thus making the house appear to be further within the estate than it really was – a necessary device on a suburban, as opposed to a rural estate. The long view from the house down the slope to Great Hockley Pool and the spires of the Birmingham churches beyond was retained, and this view, but in the opposite direction towards the house, was drawn by John Phillp (*see* Fig. 10), and later by Frances Eginton junior (*see* Fig. 11). The house was also made to appear more separate from the Manufactory than hitherto, for it now had its own entrances from the main road, rather than the carriage drive which started from the main entrance to the Manufactory. The new lengthy drives and walks, some of them within plantations and others around the pools, contributed to the effect of varied scenery and thus the illusion of greater size.

Matthew Boulton had clearly given much thought to the views to and from Soho, as shown by the evidence in his Notebook for 1795.[13] Here were listed the views from the various vantage points and including pools, hills, church spires

9 *Conjectural sketch plan of
the Soho landscape in 1809.*

10   John Phillp's view of Soho House and its parkland from Birmingham Heath, 1799.

11   View of Soho House and its parkland from Birmingham Heath, drawn and engraved by Francis Eginton junior, from Stebbing Shaw's History and Antiquities of the County of Staffordshire, vol. II, part I, 1801.

and other eye-catching buildings, such as Perrot's Folly and Aston Hall. On another page they were listed under the heading 'pictures of and from Soho'. He subsequently improved the outlook by removing trees which obstructed the view and screening unsightly buildings by planting, following his resolve to 'shut out the sight of the world and make openings to all that is pleasant and agreeable'. Examples of these observations are 'cut down the Weymouth pine and transplant the chestnut wch intercepts Bar[r] Beacon' and 'correct the trees wch intercept Handsworth Church and Mrs Walters'. He also proposed to 'make all entrances in to Soho Dark by Plantations and enter through Gothick arches made by Trees' (*see* Plate 8). Another image he wished to create was to 'surround my Farm and Works by a Garland of Flowers on one side and by an aquious mirror on the other'.

Between 1795 and 1798 Boulton directed the work of extending the gardens on the newly acquired Handsworth land, 'making an absolute fence' on all the boundaries and preparing the poor soil for planting by the methods he had perfected earlier. An illustration by Phillp shows the newly-ploughed land being rolled. By 1799, as shown on a map by map by Kempson and Robins of that date, new walks or drives had been created from the Hockley Gate entrance leading up the slope. One arm branched up as an extension of the existing Great Walk from Shell Pool.

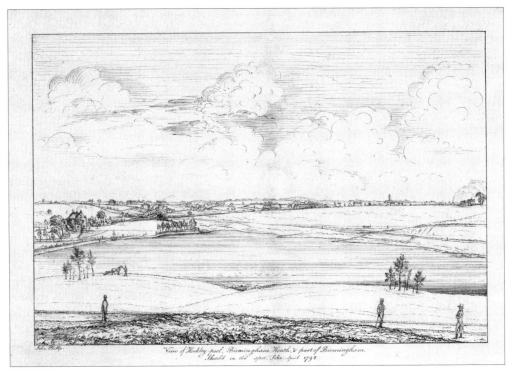

12 *John Phillp's April 1798 view from the grounds of Soho towards Birmingham, shows the newly-acquired land of Handsworth Heath being rolled after ploughing, manuring and harrowing. Boulton purchased land on Birmingham Heath, shown across the pool, in the same year.*

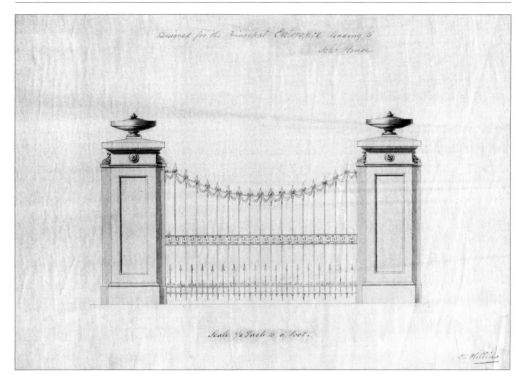

13   *William Hollins's design for the entrance to Soho House, undated.*

This was not just a gravel walk but had a green walk by its side as did the earlier path. Matthew Boulton instructed in August 1795 'when the Great Walk is staked out and the fence put up let there be a green turf walk about 3½ feet broad by the side'. As a later refinement he instructed 'plant some handsome single trees on the south side the Great Walk which make only 10 or 10½ feet wide and thus the walk will be broke by shadows'.[14] The other walk went through newly-established plantations up to the house and was known as 'the Sphinx Walk'. It joined the new carriage drive from the principal entrance on the Soho road.[15] The main entrance was probably the one designed by William Hollins as a cast iron gate hung from imposing classical piers.[16] However, Ann Watt reported to Gregory Watt in April 1796 that 'Mr B is still going on with his improvements at a great expence. The grand entrance to the house is to go from the old apple man's stall where he has already placed a bright green Gothick gate which cuts a most flaming dash', so another design for the gate may have been chosen.[17] In 1797 Hollins designed a lodge cottage, though this was not built until 1802.[18] Gravel walks were a labour intensive item to maintain and to minimise this Boulton ordered 'form gutters on each side all the walk[s] so the rain will not cut them up'.[19]

The long walk on the south-west, or far side, of Hockley Pool was completed in 1801 by extending the existing walk in the Warwickshire plantations. This walk crossed drainage channels by way of rustic bridges, Boulton noting in 1802 'improve the Grotesk bridges by branches';[20] it continued through meadow land with views across the pool towards the park and house and then went over the Great Pool dam and joined the 'Great Walk' on the other side. Boulton, now hardly able to walk, did not forgo using it, and in order to facilitate the passage of his 'chair', a single-person carriage pulled by one horse, he ordered 'lay Planks over the mill-stream and over the Tail of the Pool, so that my chair can wheel over and thereby go round the Pool'.[21]

Several new garden buildings were planned, but how many of them were built is unclear. Boulton considered acquiring a new hot house, enquiring of Samuel Wyatt in 1795 'where shall I build my Hot or greenhouse?'[22] John Rawsthorne's 1788 plan for Soho House had included an orangery and James Wyatt's 1796 scheme had an outline plan of a 'proposed greenhouse'.[23] William Hollins probably also designed an orangery for Boulton.[24] But it would appear that even by 1804 no new hot house had been built, as William Withering junior offered to sell Boulton his from his home, The Larches at Sparkbrook, 'recollecting that you have more than once made enquiry concerning such a one'.[25] Boulton considered building a temple or greenhouse facing the hermitage and its flower garden, and a 'picturesk Building', like a ruined castle, which he sketched in his notebook for 1795. However, a 'wooden house' was moved to Shell Pool in 1794. A watercolour sketch by John Phillp in 1799 may show part of the interior of this building with two recessed apertures and panelled shutters, with views of the Temple and pool on the left and on the right what may be a view of the Soho Manufactory (*see* Plate 9). This building may have started life as the bath house building which Samuel Wyatt had constructed and attached to Soho House at first-floor level some years earlier to provide the residents with a bathroom; it was not found satisfactory and Boulton subsequently had a new bathroom fitted out in a small room on the ground floor of the house. The 'wooden house' may have been moved again in 1800, from its position near the Shell Pool to the new part of the Warwickshire plantation.[26] A new boathouse was built on the causeway peninsula, and its planting and that of the island thinned so that they were more visible from various vantage points. Another boathouse was made on the Warwickshire side of Great Hockley Pool at some date after 1799. A new boat was ordered in 1800 and Cornelius Dixon was paid the very considerable sum of £82 'for painting, gilding and ornamenting' it in 1805, presumably including the Boulton crest as on an earlier boat sketched by John Phillp in 1796 (*see* Fig. 16).[27] For this boat a more robust boathouse was constructed than the simple wooden structures shown in several Phillp illustrations. It was built in 1801 using brick and had 'oak gothic doors'[28] and these doors may be the ones Phillp sketched (*see* Plate 10), or perhaps designed. It was surrounded by a plantation. The location of the boathouse is undocumented but it may have been at the far end of Great Hockley Pool, where a boathouse is shown on Snape's plan of 1820 (*see* Fig. 34, p.63) and which in the tithe apportionment of 1847 is described as 'Boathouse Piece'.

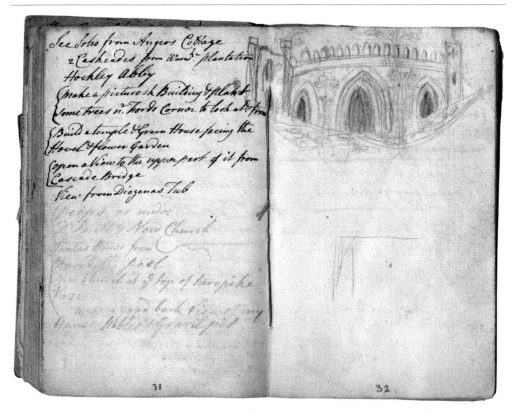

14   *Pages from Matthew Boulton's Garden Notebook for 1795 showing the views he wished to create and his sketch for a proposed 'picturesk building', but there is no evidence that this was ever built.*

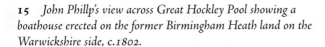

15   *John Phillp's view across Great Hockley Pool showing a boathouse erected on the former Birmingham Heath land on the Warwickshire side, c.1802.*

16 *Matthew Robinson Boulton's boat with the Boulton crest on the stern, by John Phillp, 1796.*

In the pleasure grounds in proximity to the house Matthew Boulton placed several pieces of statuary including a number of vases on plinths and a pair of stone sphinxes, also on plinths, that were put up by Hollins in September 1795.[29] The sphinxes and three stone vases had been supplied from London by Edward Gray Saunders at a cost of £30 and a further £17 for the making of packing cases and transport by canal to the Soho wharf.[30] The sphinxes were placed near the house at the start of a new walk, which became known as 'the Sphinx Walk', which ran parallel to the turnpike road and led to the new kitchen garden.[31] John Phillp made a measured drawing of one of the sphinxes in 1796. One of the vases was placed to good advantage on a prominence at the back of the house, also sketched by Phillp (*see* Plate 11). James Watt's wife, Annie, was scornful of what she saw as Boulton's latest excesses, writing to her son Gregory:

> Mr Boulton is going on in spending money. He is now narrowing his broad Gravel walks and has placed two Gigantic Synphaxes [*sic*] near the house. He is increasing the number of his carriages amazingly. Last night he got a new one with some kind of new screws, *springs* I mean. He has now a coach 2 post chaises a Yarmouth car and 2 kinds of Garden chairs. I believe he is gone crazy.[32]

A lamp pedestal with a lamp iron was put up in 1796, supplied by Hollins, and a second one was put up in front of the house by Wyatt in 1798.[33] These may have been put up as a pair on either side of the drive, as they appear in a late 19th-century photograph of Soho House (*see* Fig. 39, p.75).

Once he had bought the freehold Boulton was able to landscape extensively at the rear of the house for the first time and plan the views from the back windows. The wall on the old boundary was pulled down and the original roadway to the Manufactory, which subsequently had become a footpath, known as the 'hollow way', was retained as a drive to the new stables. A lawn was made beyond it, and in 1795 he decided to plant 'trees and shrubs at the back of the intended stables upon the back lawn and upon the slope of hill so as not to obstruct the view of the Pool from the house and view it from Birmingham Heath'.[34] The new stables were built in 1798-1800 by Benjamin Wyatt, builder, of Sutton Coldfield, well separated from the house (*see* Fig. 19). They replaced the stable block at right angles to the service wing, which had been built in 1770 and extended in 1785.[35] The demolition of the old stable block allowed for further extensions of the house. William Hollins designed the new stables in 1797 as a principal block facing a lesser range enclosing a courtyard.[36] The blind arcading of the principal block echoed the detailing on Soho House, whilst its central cupola and dovecote was reminiscent of the centre of the Principal Building of the Manufactory. However, Matthew Boulton did not wish to see the stable yard from the house and in March 1798 ordered the gardener to put 'particularly good

17　*Measured drawing by John Phillp in 1796 of one of the pair of sphinxes bought the previous year.*

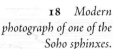

18　*Modern photograph of one of the Soho sphinxes.*

19   *John Phillp's sketch of 1799 of the new stables at Soho, designed by William Hollins.*

20   *View of the sheep netting erected in 1795;*
this divided the lawn, set with irregular shaped
beds, from the park used for grazing the stock of the
hobby farm. John Phillp, 1801.

soil where the trees are to be planted to stop up the view of the stable yard'.[37]

At the front of the house the area of lawn was extended and had beds of mixed planting inserted in it, together with 'handsome single trees'. A new net and chain fence 504 yards (460.86 metres) long kept out grazing animals. This was probably installed in 1795 when Boulton had noted 'sheep netting in London at Davison in Fish Street Hill and Ulstomins at Fleet Street selling at about 7d per square yards.'[38] In 1802 a system of trellis for growing climbers was supplied for the new façade of the house by Cornelius Dixon.[39] There were many new garden seats including two with Chinese backs supplied by Benjamin Wyatt in 1799.[40]

21   *John Phillp's view of the new gateway to the Manufactory terrace, from a design for a proposed medal, c.1797.*

Matthew Boulton also gave thought to the landscaping around the Manufactory. In 1795 he decided to 'Form the Terras at the front of the Manufactory so as to be always clean and neat'.[41] A new retaining wall was built and the ground levelled and then gravelled. In 1797 he decided to 'put a good pale fence by the side of the road and down to the manufactory'[42] and the rather informal five-barred gates were replaced by metal gates and gate piers. Boulton also planted on the steep slope of his own land overlooking the Manufactory, having posed himself the question, 'How shall I form my Western ground to be handsome in the sight of those going to the manufactory?'[43] (*see* Plate 8).

From 1794 Anne Boulton was hampered by a knee injury (sustained falling down the coach steps in the dark) from making her usual visits to friends, and over the next few years was restricted to spending much time at Soho, undergoing a variety of uncomfortable treatments aimed at getting her mobile again. During this period the garden provided her with a degree of interest and pleasure, which can be glimpsed in letters to and from her father. In April 1801 Matthew Boulton wrote to his daughter:

> I am persuaded that if one of my chairs was placed upon the Lawn with a cushion in it and a proper footstool you might be carried into it and wheel'd about upon the grass lawn without the least injury from shakeing: pray try it and do not loose the benefit of this fine spring weather.[44]

On 9 June the same year, Boulton's personal clerk William Cheshire reported to Matthew Boulton on his daughter's health, and provided a picture of all the various activities in maintaining the gardens:

The gardener's people are now so spread over your gardens, pleasure grounds, and plantations that it is not easy to describe their various operations. Mowing, cleaning, weeding, and gravelling form the chief part of their present daily occupations. It is to be regretted that you are not here to enjoy this most delightful season. Your plantations and lawns are now more picturesque than ever. I have the pleasure to say that Miss Boulton enjoys remarkably good spirits.[45]

By 19 June Anne was venturing further from the house and wished to go on the lake in the new boat, the difficulty being getting in and out of it. Her father wrote:

I shall order every part of the road round the garden to be Roll'd as smooth as possible that you may be induced to live in the open air as much as possible it being the next best thing to the sea breezes. I also approve of the Swing and the Boat, but some very commodious means must be contrived to place you in and take you out without the least risk danger or pain.[46]

The second phase of landscaping involved the purchase of very large quantities of plants, particularly trees, which Boulton continued to buy from the local firm of Brunton and Forbes almost exclusively up to 1798. He then switched to the new partnership of Brunton and Hunter but also bought from others, including a Wolverhampton nurseryman, William Lowe, between 1802 and 1806. He knew well what nurseries there were, and in 1801 ordered the gardener to inspect their stock and collect a gift from Samuel Galton: 'Trees must be had, as follows, Mr Galton will give me Scotch Firs which are at Worley [Warley] and near there lives Mr Hunter a Nursery Man see what he has Mr Blakesley of Bordesley, beyond Deritend, he is a Nursery Man. See Nursery at Warstone Lane'.[47] This was to obtain trees for the extension to the Warwickshire plantation, where he had decided to use 'quick hedge, Scotch Firs, 2 sorts spruce, some larches, 2 sorts chestnuts, Beeches, oaks, elms, sycamores, Birches, mountain ash, poplers' – the latter were balsam, cassady and Lombardy poplars. He also used a new conifer, the Chinese Abor-vitae (*Thuja orientalis*) and walnuts. 'Quicks', or hawthorn, was used to augment any new post and rail fence. Although earlier he had used conifers extensively, the emphasis was nevertheless predominantly on deciduous trees, even for the deep boundary plantings, to blot out unsightly buildings as an earlier list indicates. A list headed 'Plant in Octr next 1795' consisted of 'white poplers, Birches, Horse chestnuts elms and many high trees opposite Gratrix[,] planes, Hornbeam, Beech, Limes, Seccamores variegated, purple Beech'.[48] In 1801 he had decided to 'plant poplars at the back of Great Pool Dam'.[49] Elms were extensively planted on the outlying land let as farms and in the plantations of Thornhill, the nearby house Boulton bought from John Scale, originally at his son's request.[50]

Less evidence survives as to the shrubs used but they included laburnums, Italian privet, Portuguese laurels, and Persian lilac, and in January 1798 William

Lowe supplied 65 honeysuckles in five varieties and a quantity of roses. The honeysuckles were 'early Dutch' (*Lonicera periclymenum* 'Belgica'), 'early flowering' (? *L.caprifolium*), 'late white', 'late strip'd' and 'oak leav'd'. At this period they were not used as climbers but were grown running along the ground. The roses included 'Blush 100 leav'd Province' (*Rosa centifolia*), 'Rose Mundie' (*Rosa mundi*) and 'Red Belgic rose'.[51] More roses were ordered in 1799 from J. Blaksley, who supplied '10 roses (choice pots)'.[52] These may have been used in 'the oval', a bed at the back of the house where in 1798 Boulton had decided to 'put a few pretty bushy low shrubs' and to surround it with posts and bars. At the same time he decided to plant round the lamp pedestals – 'join by planting the large Firs on each side the pedestal'.[53] More shrubs were used at Shell Pool, Boulton having decided in January 1801 'to dress up the outside of the Shell Pool dam and plant laurels and other evergreen shrubs amongst the trees'.[54] Annual flowers continued to be an important part of the Soho 'garland of flowers', but there were never enough to satisfy Boulton as the following entries from the Notebook for 1801-03 indicate:

22 June 1801	Q[uer]y is it too late to sow <u>more</u> flowers. Next year we should grow many more flowers
28 March 1802	better soil, muck, marl and more Flowers particularly French marygolds …
28 April 1802	Sow French marygolds Sow others that are not too late

A particular problem in establishing trees on a major scale was that of watering them, and Boulton applied technology to the problem. In 1796 he started using the power of the Mint's steam engine connected to a pump to water trees and his new lawns. He wrote to James Wyatt in July 1796:

the beauty of my place depends much upon my walks being clean and neat and my lawns green, which they will be hereafter as I have brought Hockley Brook up to 4 feet above my parlour and I can flood my whole premises.[55]

The water was conveyed in elm pipes to where it was needed and Boulton's private account was charged for the use of 'the flooding machine', as the Mint engine in this capacity was termed. In 1797 he spent £65 on its use.[56] A further innovation was to use the Mint engine with extra piping to extend the watering operations further. William Cheshire reported in August 1800:

The new piping for your Fire Engine being arriv'd we are able to avail ourselves of the use of that powerful machine in watering the Lawns at the front and back of your house and all those trees in the vicinity that are inaccessible to the Flooding Machine. The Fire Engine was thus employ'd from sun-set on Saturday Evening 'till 10 o'clock, and the whole of yesterday and today and finding that the gardener could not employ additional people in watering by hand where necessary for want of a water cart I have procured one on hire from Birmingham.[57]

In the new Warwickshire Plantation on the opposite side of the pool, which was well out of reach of the Mint engine, Boulton planned to use a modified beam pump to water the trees in 1801, a drawing of which together with numerous calculations appeared in his notebook.[58]

Boulton's concern for his young trees is evident in many letters: 'I am glad to find that the gardener has not spared watering the trees which Mr Watt informs me grow very well', he wrote to his daughter in May 1801, and a month later, 'What is the news with you? Do my young Trees grow? Has James Duncan connected the pump w[i]th the Mint Engine?'[59]

A ram pump was installed in the garden in 1798[60] and several wells were sunk, and in 1803 Boulton turned to the services of a 'drownder' or water diviner, so great was the requirement for water for household, Manufactory and garden.[61]

The increase in size of the gardens enabled Matthew Boulton to lay out a new and much larger kitchen garden in 1800, choosing a distant part of the estate near the Soho turnpike, and retaining two old cottages for estate workmen. The extent of the new kitchen garden was not fixed for some time, and in January 1801 Boulton decided on 'a temporary augmentation of the kitchen garden' and that 'the entrance into the top of the kitchen garden must be through a close fence and a door so as not to see the necessary [the lavatory]'.[62] Even in 1809, just before Boulton died, the layout was not fixed and a newly-engaged gardener wanted a decision: 'lest the family should be disappointed he begs to suggest the cropping of such parts of the present garden ground as will least interfere with your views in the new arrangement with Pease, Beans …'.[63] The new garden was partly walled, perhaps on the road boundary, and surrounded by a hedge. The decision to relocate the kitchen garden was followed by the pulling down of the fruit wall near the Manufactory and the removal of the land on which it stood, which was added to the Little Hockley Pool.

Matthew Boulton also allocated a portion of his Soho estate for 'guinea gardens' which were rented by his tenants and workmen, in the newly-purchased Warwickshire land beyond the engine yard. Birmingham was noted by the 18th century for the quantity of guinea gardens, rather like today's allotments, that were available at a rent of a guinea (£1 1s.) a year in many areas of Birmingham and which enabled town dwellers without gardens to cultivate land for pleasure and profit. Boulton had previously leased land as detached gardens for his workmen on outlying portions of his land, but was now able to offer his tenants land in a more convenient location. Twenty-four gardens were laid out at the end of April 1801 to a plan drawn by John Phillp for Boulton, who was anxious that the land should be divided as equally as possible; 'Snape's man' was therefore paid for setting them out,[64] each comprising an eighth of an acre. Every garden was accessed from a walk wide enough for a wheel barrow, and Boulton had offered to help 'the garden speculators' by 'ploughing, cross ploughing, harrowing and cross harrowing' the land, but William Cheshire said 'they wished to avail themselves of the present season' and would double-dig it themselves, wanting the equivalent of ploughing costs in manure. But Cheshire countered that 'manure is of greater value to you than money'.[65] The names of the tenants are visible on the plan and 'after Mr Brusch [a diesinker at the Mint] had made his election of three gardens, the remainder of us drew lots and the numbers drawn determined the order of choosing'.[66]

The purchasing of the Soho estate led to changes in Matthew Boulton's farming activities, probably increasing the scale of his operations but, more significantly, the location. Whereas previously he had farmed on rented outlying parcels of land, he now farmed his own land and the farm mostly formed part of the grounds of Soho. At its height the Soho homestead, as it was called, was 53 acres. It comprised

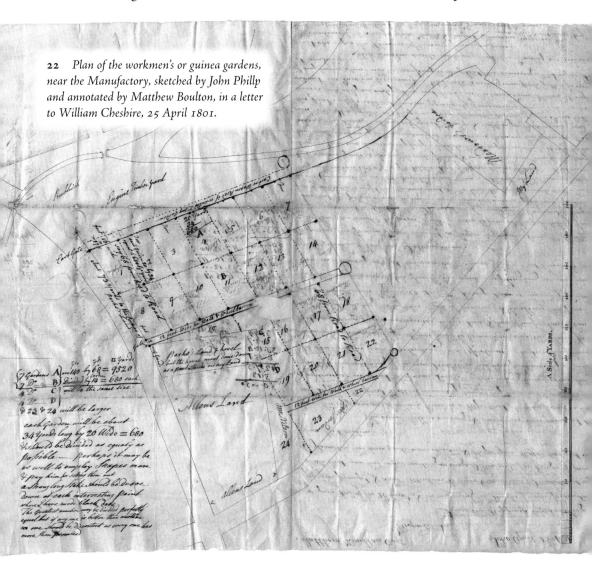

22   *Plan of the workmen's or guinea gardens, near the Manufactory, sketched by John Phillp and annotated by Matthew Boulton, in a letter to William Cheshire, 25 April 1801.*

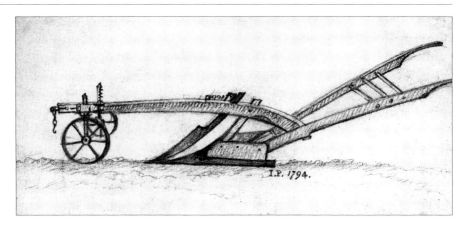

23   *Drawing by John Phillp of a turn-wrest plough used at Soho, 1794.*

two fields on the far side of the Soho turnpike – Stoney Field and Rickyard Piece, fields on either side of the mill pool, parkland at the front and back of the house and meadow land on both sides of the Hockley Pools. Boulton, always ready to extend his knowledge, noted in 1795 under the heading 'Books on agriculture wanted,' 'Wright on Watering Meadows' and 'Davies on Watering Meadows', so perhaps these meadows were flooded from the pool with a view to improving the quality of the pasture and providing spring grazing. In 1797 the farm was producing barley, oats, clover, potatoes and turnips,[67] and grazing for a variety of live-stock including carriage and riding horses, working horses, pigs, sheep and dairy cows. Poultry was also kept, with ducks and swans gracing the pools. In 1802 Boulton recorded in a notebook (no. 92) that he had four cows, two horses, a pony and a team of four cart horse, and that his son had six horses.

It is evident that the setting up and running of the farm was very much Boulton's concern, although his daughter took an interest in the animals. Writing to Anne, who was with friends in Brighthelmston [Brighton] in September 1800, her father concluded, 'Soho looks as verdant as in the Spring and Dash [the dog], the Cows, the Sheep and the Horses are all well'.[68] If Boulton was away he was kept fully informed by William Cheshire: 'The gardener has spread the mud on the new trenched land and will prepare it as you direct for turnips – your team is diminished in strength by the loss of your Horse Redman, who died of an inflamatory disorder a few days ago', he reported in June 1801.[69] As each parcel of land was acquired it was brought into cultivation as Boulton decreed; thus for the Stoney Piece purchased in 1799 he directed, 'Remove ½ the stone to the nearest corner and other ½ to Grices Corner plow the Land and carry on black soil carry in Lime plow and mix and in Winter marl'.[70] It is not clear where the farm buildings were, although they may have been in the 'rick yard piece' across the Soho road, and piggeries were built as part of the new stables. The homestead was a hobby operation and an amenity and did not make a profit. In 1805 the annual cost of running it and the kitchen garden was £900, while the estimated value of the crops produced was £667.[71] In 1806, because Matthew Boulton's sharply declining health did not allow him to direct the farm, the acreage was reduced by letting some of the land and much of the farm equipment was sold. This including a chaff cutting and a winnowing machine, a plough and a cart with gearing and the hames, traces and harness for three draft horses which were sold.[72]

The labour bill for the enlarged garden and farm was a not insignificant item of expenditure. In 1806 the new gardener estimated that 11 people were required at a cost of over £327 per annum:

> For keeping in order the kitchen Ground, Flower Borders and walks and for mowing the lawn and verges the Gardener is of opinion it will require 2 Labourers, 1 Lad and 2 women – the walk round the Great Pool not to be included …

> For keeping in order all the Farm Land Mr Boulton now occupies the Gardener is of opinion it will require 3 Labourers, a carter and a Plough Boy; but that more will be necessary during the Hay and Corn Harvests.[73]

To ascertain the price that should be paid for mowing and haymaking Boulton had consulted his business partner, James Watt, and noted:

> Mr Watt pd for mowing in 1800
>   for meadow grass sans drink 4s per acre
>   for ditto in 1801 no drink 4/6 per acre
>   for clover 1802 ditto 3/6
> Haymaking 1s per day and at the end of the Harvest a supper, drink and 1s each over.[74]

This reflects the sharp rise in bread prices, and therefore wages, which had taken place since 1797 when a mower could be got for 2s. a day.[75]

The new gardener's salary in 1806 was £54 12s. per annum, as befitted the level of his responsibilities. In the 1790s Boulton had employed two gardeners on half this wage each, so it was probably necessary to pay much more to get a superior man who, as Boulton put it in 1805, would not need directing, 'which the infirm state of my health will not allow me to do … neither is it possible for my son to pay much attention to it as he has already too much business of importance upon his hands.'[76] Matthew Robinson Boulton did, however, get involved with the garden from time to time. In 1807, when he had been seriously ill with a fever, his father (who was also unwell) wrote with the help of William Cheshire to a Mr Robinson (possibly John Robinson, a relative who worked in the London banking house), that 'In fine weather my Son now amuses himself with Garden Improvements, which is a good species of recreation, and will, I hope, firmly re-establish his health.'[77]

Only exceptionally were the grounds of Soho opened to the general public, perhaps the only recorded occasion during Matthew Boulton's lifetime being the celebrations for the Peace of Amiens in April 1802 when:

24   *Sketch of a cow under a larch tree at Soho by John Phillp, c.1801.*

early in the afternoon the road from the town was crowded with passengers – the gates of the garden were thrown open, and gave admittance to thousands of spectators, of whom it is but justice to observe such was their orderly behaviour, that they departed almost without breaking either shrub or tree, or doing any damage.

The house was adorned on the summit of the roof by a magnificent star, composed of variegated lamps, and the centre window was embellished by a beautiful transparency in glass of a female figure, in the attitude of offering a thanksgiving for the return of peace. The manufactory was illuminated throughout its spacious front with upwards of 2,600 coloured lamps …[78]

Matthew Boulton died on 17 August 1809, his work on Soho complete. Through his persistence, flair and artistic vision he had created a setting for his manufactories and his home that excelled that of other industrialists. An American visitor in 1776 had observed the combination of *Dulce* and *Utile* in his landscaping, whilst a visitor in 1802 considered that:

> The different features of the place form a striking fine whole, both grand and beautiful; the more interesting when we consider that it is entirely the creation of modern years, formed by the continued operation of taste, science and wealth, out of a desolate heath inhabited only by a colony of rabbits.[79]

Erasmus Darwin's more poetic description of Soho would also suggest that Boulton achieved his objectives:

> No expense has been spared to render these works uniform and handsome in architecture as well as great and commodious. The same liberal spirit and taste has the great and worthy proprietor gradually exercised in the adjoining gardens, groves and pleasure grounds; which at the same time that they form an agreeable separation from his own residence render Soho a much admired scene of picturesque beauty. Wandering thro' these secluded walks and on the bank of the several fine lakes and waterfalls which adorn them we may here enjoy the sweets of solitude and retirement.[80]

Three

Soho through the Eyes of John Phillp

Val Loggie[1]

The greatest number of known views of the Soho estate and Manufactory were produced by John Phillp (*c.*1778-1815).[2] Many of his sketches and watercolours, mainly of the 1790s, were later collected together in an album which has been known, since it was presented to Birmingham Museums & Art Gallery by a descendant of Phillp, as 'the Phillp album' (*see* below). John Phillp came to Soho from Cornwall in 1793, when he was about fourteen, but as the dated material in the album begins in 1792 it is clear that he was already painting in watercolour before he came to Soho.

A letter from George C. Fox, a Quaker copper merchant, to Matthew Boulton told him that 'the poor Lad who thee wert so very kind as to permit me to place under thy Friendly protection is arrived thus farr [Bath] in his journey to Birmingham, and I intend to forward him in a few days. As we look upon him to be a prudent steady boy I trust he will do every thing to give thee satisfaction – his name is John Phillp.'[3] Boulton replied that the work he had intended for Phillp when they had discussed the matter in Falmouth was now discontinued 'on acct of ye unfortunate rupture with France, & I now have no species of Painting done in my Manufacture: however I will find out what sort of employment is best suited for his talents.'[4] Fox put the boy on a Bristol coach on 2 March and he was expected to arrive at Birmingham the following week.[5]

By September, Fox was writing of 'thy very kind attention to John Phillp, who [I] hope will continue to do *his utmost* to merit the continuance of thy Friendship, & to evince his gratitude for thy protection & patronage, which we are satisfied will enable him to provide for himself in a few years, *if he conducts himself with propriety*, which we shall be glad to learn – we shall be obliged by remembering us to him, & to tell him that we should be glad to receive a few lines from him.'[6] It is not clear why either Fox or Boulton took such an interest in John Phillp. Phillp family tradition suggests that the boy was in fact Boulton's illegitimate son, the product of a liaison when the latter was in Cornwall on engine business.[7] However, there appears to be no firm evidence for this,[8] and it may simply be, as Brian Gould suggests, that Boulton treated Phillp well due to his talent, rather than to any kind of relationship; Gould argues that Phillp's position was on a par with 'a favoured servant, or at best that of one or two of the sons of Boulton's managers, in whose education Boulton also took a personal interest.'[9]

It was not unusual for Boulton to encourage young men who displayed some artistic talent. He himself had been taught to draw as a young man and had long been aware of the importance of artists, writing to James Adam in 1770, 'I have trained up and am training up more young plain Country Lads, all of which that betray any genius are taught to draw from which I derive many advantages that are not to be found in any manufacture that is or can be established in a great & debauched Capital.'[10] This was a long-term policy, for setting down thoughts on the best way to go about setting up a button manufactory, during a visit to Paris in 1786 (when he may have been asked for advice on the subject), Boulton wrote 'The best way to have good artists is to train up young men of abilities & to have them under contract for 7 years at least – If these young men are of the lower Class provided they are of decent families they will do better than those who may aspire to be Gentlemen.'[11] He also worked extensively with established architects like James Adams' brother, Robert, William Chambers and various members of the Wyatt family. In the 1760s Boulton and Fothergill had employed a 'Mr Green', probably Benjamin Green, to produce engravings of some of their products which could be shown to potential customers.[12] Artists, or those with a good pen, were needed not just in the more obvious areas of manufacture like silver, ormolu and medals but also to produce the working drawings for steam engines.

Matthew Boulton had previously worked closely with Francis Eginton (1737-1805) who was probably working at Soho by 1764 as a chaser and engraver. By the 1770s he was referred to as Boulton and Fothergill's chief designer and was travelling to London on their behalf, looking for design ideas, visiting members of the aristocracy and architects and assisting with the sale of Soho products at the auctions held at Christie and Ansell's salerooms. Eginton was also encouraged to work in other artistic areas, including experimenting with aquatint and the development of mechanical paintings. This last venture was not a financial success and Eginton left Soho in 1781, becoming well known as a glass painter.[13] It seems likely that in Phillp, Boulton had hoped to finally find a replacement for Eginton.[14] He had employed other artists such as the diesinkers J.P. Droz and C.H. Küchler at Soho, but these had proved difficult relationships and the opportunity to train and influence an artist whose loyalty would lie with Boulton and Soho must have been one that appealed to Boulton.[15]

A bill dated 30 June 1795 shows that Phillp received instruction in architectural drawing from William Hollins, at a cost of 15s. per quarter for four quarters.[16] Hollins (1763-1843) was a sculptor, stonemason and architect who worked for

Boulton on the improvements at Soho House. He established his own practice in Birmingham in 1798; he also founded a Drawing Academy in Great Charles Street, which re-opened in 1801 after he had purchased a large collection of casts, prints and drawings.[17] Architectural drawing, with its need for precision and detail, would have been a useful skill at the Manufactory as many of the techniques could be transferred to design drawings. Hollins's tuition seems to have had a strong influence on Phillp, whose depiction of buildings is carefully observed and detailed.

Phillp also appears to have received some instruction from the Birmingham landscape painter Joseph Barber (1757-1811) in 1796, as two watercolours in the Phillp album are inscribed '1st under IB IP 1796' and '2 C.F. IB 1796'.[18] It is likely that IB is Barber and C.F. is 'copied from'. Barber certainly had links with Boulton and Soho; he had taught the Watt children and someone at Soho House, probably Anne Boulton, and produced a view of Soho House and estate for *The Tablet*, a diary featuring views of gentlemen's houses.[19] No bill has been found for any tuition which might suggest that it was something Phillp had arranged for himself. It was common practice at this time to receive specialist instruction from various

25 *Sketch of Soho Manufactory by John Phillp, with trees added by Amos Green, c.1797-9.*

drawing masters in different areas of expertise and Phillp seems to have taken the opportunity to seek advice from other artists whenever possible – one view of the Manufactory has 'trees by Amos Green York', a watercolour artist who had known Boulton in his youth (*see* Fig. 25).[20]

It is also possible that Phillp took some instruction from the landscape painter Robert Andrew Riddell, as many of his views of the estate are dated 1796, when Riddell also produced a series of views of Soho. Riddell wrote to Boulton on 15 June 1796:

> I have taken the earliest opportunity of sending the views of Soho, which I hope you will approve of, I can assure you every care has been taken to render them as agreeable as possible and make every variety that the scenes would admit of.
>
> In the view made to suggest the improvements, you'll observe that simplicity is particularly attended to and can easily be accomplished in nature, the places planted with shrubs are purposely to break the lines of formality, and hide the stalks of the fir trees which give the scene a bare dry look, and to break the edge of the ford when seen from the windows of the house &c. I think the break in the hill when the sand has been dug adds to the beauty of the place and will moreso if there is an ash & Oak tree planted in it, you often perceive such places
>
> [...] I have not finished the other drawing wherein the new house was to have been placed but that I can do at any time whenever the plann is finished. I will be your way in Septr next when I will put in the trees you have planted, on the corner before the house.[21]

Evidently Riddell was not merely producing views of Soho as it then was, but also suggesting improvements. He charged five guineas each for the seven views he had completed. The unfinished drawing was awaiting the completion of James Wyatt's designs for remodelling the house, work on which began later that summer.[22] It is possible that the seven completed views and the one he had not finished corresponded to the list of eight pictures of and from Soho listed in Boulton's 1795 notebook.[23] If Riddell's views have survived their present whereabouts is unknown.

Phillp was sent to London in 1802 where he visited the studios of artists, purchased reference material and saw the Royal Academy exhibition.[24] In 1805 he again went to London to visit the home of connoisseur Thomas Hope and sketch some of his collection to provide models for designs at Soho.[25] As Phillp matured and his skills improved, he undertook design work for the Mint and the plated ware company, as well as a range of other roles including supervising the library and wine cellar at Soho House and drawing plans.[26] By 1807 a separate room was set aside for him to work in, where models and designs could be 'made, preservd and properly class'd'.[27]

Phillp and his artistic skills were important to Soho. Richard Chippendall (principal London agent of the Plated Company) wrote in 1808:

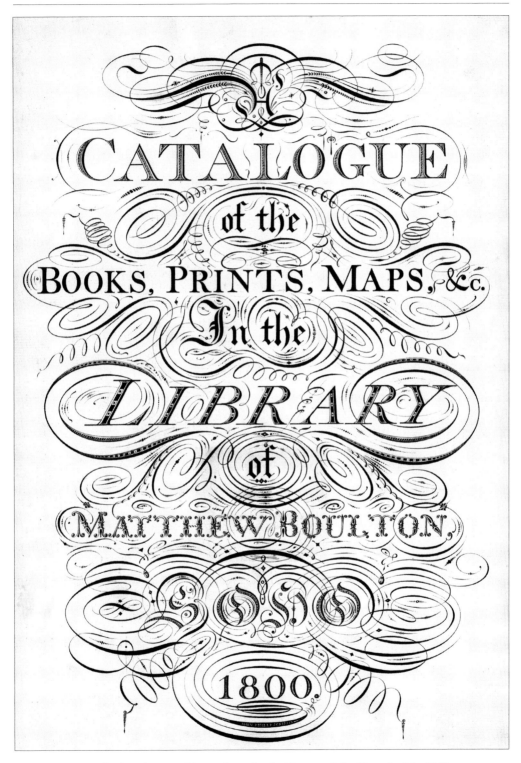

26 *Design for the title page of the catalogue for the library at Soho House by John Phillp, 1800.*

It has given me some uneasiness in understanding from Mr Lawson that Mr Phillp's health is in such a precarious state; the loss of such a pencil as his wou'd be felt and not easily be replaced. Those at Soho feel not its effects perhaps so immediately as myself; and I can easily see how advisable it wou'd be for some youth to have the advantage of his instruction and can only lament the difficulty and delicacy in such a matter, which I forsee have obstacles not easily to be surmounted.[28]

Phillp continued in poor health until his death in 1815.

His sketches and watercolours around Soho provide the most detailed information we have about the garden, the buildings and the surrounding landscape. The album at Birmingham Museums & Art Gallery which contains the majority of this work is likely to have been put together by a later family member. It is not arranged chronologically and much of it is undated, the dated items running from 1792[29] to 1811, the majority clustered from 1795 to 1805. A later insert is signed and dated 'C. Phillp 1830' and another 'C.E. Phillp 1854'. It is possible that this is the person who put the album together. Sketches, finished works and rough studies were mounted with no apparent order or respect for the numbering system evident on some of the material. Conservation work undertaken on the contents, which included their removal from the album due to the acidity of its pages, enabled the backs of images to be examined for the first time, which brought to light two additional drawings, dates, captions and other information that had previously been hidden.[30] When the material was mounted in the album no additional annotation or labelling was undertaken, so the only titles we have are Phillp's own, which are limited. The location of some views has been determined through research and comparison, but some remain to be identified while others may be imaginary or copies of other artists' work.[31]

Additional Phillp images have come to light via other branches of the family since Soho House opened to the public and it is likely that more remain to be found, but the known topographical views relating to Soho are currently concentrated in the Phillp album. The collection has been used extensively in research work by Phillada Ballard on the garden and estate, the results of which can be seen in this volume, and by George Demidowicz in his work on the Manufactory and Mint which is in preparation.[32] Both studies are much the richer for the survival of this material.

Phillp supplies us with more detail on the estate at Soho than any other artist, presumably because he had greater access and knew the site so well. His work provides more information on the surroundings of the Manufactory than any other, as well as a number of views of the parkland and garden buildings. In the album there were eight views showing the Manufactory, in several of which it appears in the background rather than as the main subject. One is now lost and is known only as a reverse (white on black) copy taken when the album was lent to Birmingham Library in 1930 by Phillp's descendants.[33] All of his dated views which include the Manufactory were carried out in 1796. Three of these 1796 views are numbered: 'No 1 sketch', '2', and 'No 3 S' (presumably sketch). Other items in the album are also numbered but the numbers on sketches and finished works do not correspond. In general, watercolours seem to have numbers implying they are finished, while pen and ink or pen and wash views tend to be labelled sketch. Three of the Manufactory views are undated, unlabelled and appear to be even rougher sketches. There is also a view of Soho Foundry dated 1795, the year it was built, and there are two views of the Mint presses and the ceiling to the coining room, dated 1799.

Phillp's depictions of the Soho Manufactory include an unfinished version of a view of the Principal Building with Rolling Mill Row to the right and the mill pool in the foreground (*see* Fig. 25, p.45). This is the most common viewpoint for images of the Principal Building and the one which would have been seen by most visitors as they approached from the Handsworth turnpike. In constructing the Principal Building, Boulton had ensured that the first view of his Manufactory was of an impressive building which resembled a country house rather than a manufactory and it was a view of this building that was most often selected for depiction until well after Boulton's death.[34]

There are two finished watercolours of 1796 with part of the Manufactory building visible in the background. One shows a view looking from the old stables and water trough out towards Thornhill House, with the mill pool and the top of the Principal Building visible in the middle ground and is numbered '1' (*see* Plate 11). The other watercolour is from Soho Pool looking towards the smaller-scale buildings at the side of the Manufactory, with the vegetation on either side of the pool acting as side screens and a family of ducks to give interest in the foreground (*see* Plate 4). It is numbered '2', suggesting that these are two of a proposed series. Neither has a caption explaining what they show and this has been deduced from other evidence. Both views appear to be predominantly concerned with topographical recording but include more sophisticated artistic techniques like aerial perspective and repoussoir to create depth in the image.[35] The images focus on the parkland with the Manufactory buildings merely forming part of the backdrop. Image '1' in particular looks out across the back lawn of the Soho estate to farmland and a number of buildings scattered across the landscape. It includes a classical urn on a grassy knoll, emphasising the sophistication of the gardens.

A pen and ink view with an ink wash also shows the Soho Pool looking towards the Manufactory, but from further back and to the left, allowing the boathouse to be included (*see* Fig. 27). The boathouse and surrounding foliage are the focus of attention and receive the colour wash, while the Manufactory building and fruit wall form a backdrop to the right. It is labelled '1796/Sketch taken on the spot at SOHO J Phillp 1796 No 3 S'. Although made on the spot this is a confident sketch with crisp, clean lines to the building. The vegetation fills the image, the sky being reduced to the top right hand corner above the buildings.

A pen and ink drawing, annotated 'View of the SOHO MANU-FACTORY taken from Birmingham Heath/July 1796 J Phillp Fecit No 1 Sketch' is a different view from that labelled '1' above. It looks north from the heath and shows the Manufactory from the rear among trees. It makes clear the extent of the wooded setting of the Manufactory; the house, on top of the hill, was quite shielded from the factory and cannot be seen for the trees. None of the published views of the Manufactory at the time show this wooded aspect; not until the 1830s, when the site was portrayed from the back, would this be so apparent.[37] The heath itself occupies the foreground, so that the area of interest is compressed into a narrow horizontal band.

From the available evidence, the lost sketch appears to be a very rough undated

27 *Soho Pool with boathouse and Soho Manufactory, by John Phillp, 1796.*

28 *View of Soho Manufactory taken from Birmingham Heath by John Phillp, 1796.*

line drawing of the side of the Principal Building and Rolling Mill Row, taken from the side of the mill pool. It depicts this side of the Manufactory almost square-on which is unusual (it was usually shown obliquely, with the focus on the Principal Building which allowed the artist to emphasise the scale of the site and show that the Principal Building was not just a façade). The image appears to be pencil, but this may be a softening effect of the 1930 copying technique. It has a frame drawn around it and there is a line of writing above the frame which it is not possible to read. This sketch is particularly notable for the large number of chimneys and tops of buildings shown behind Rolling Mill Row, perhaps an indication of what was actually there but the complexity of which led the artist to abandon the work.

It is likely that this was a first draft of the surviving pen and ink drawing labelled 'View of the Soho Manufactory taken on the spot John Phillp Fecit 1796' (*see* Fig. 29). It takes a slightly different viewpoint, even more square on, simplifying and eliminating the buildings and chimneys behind. It allows the buildings to run out of the right-hand side of the frame (in the earlier version more of the buildings were included) and adds the wooded hill to the left. Once again the sky forms the top half of the picture and water occupies much of the foreground, restricting the interest to a narrow band. However, the edge of the pool and a path lie on the left-hand side of the image and act as a side screen, helping to create depth and lead the eye into the picture.

The final image is very different. In pen and ink it shows the Principal Building at its usual angle but closer than other views, avoiding including the adjacent buildings. It is enclosed in a circular frame with a blank section at the bottom and a border above as if leaving space for a date (*see* Fig. 21, p.35). This suggests that this is a design for a medal. The penmanship is less precise and there is a great deal of use of cross hatching to show shadow and to suggest the water of the canal in the foreground. The work is unsigned and although it is not a characteristic Phillp drawing, it probably is by him, as there are other examples of his work which display a looser technique or which use cross hatching. It is possible that this drawing was simply an exercise; there is a design for a banknote in the album but no suggestion that there were ever any plans for involvement in their design and

29   *'View of the Soho Manufactory, taken on the Spot' by John Phillp, 1796.*

production at Soho. Alternatively, it could be a proposal for Matthew Boulton's memorial medal which was distributed by Phillp at his funeral.

There are three distant Phillp views of Soho House, all from the far side of Soho Pool showing it perched on top of the hill. This view of the house from across the pool was how it was most commonly shown; the engraving after Joseph Barber in *The Tablet* of 1796, and the view by Francis Eginton junior in Stebbing Shaw's *History of Staffordshire* of 1801 both use this angle. Two of Phillp's watercolours of 1796 show the house before Wyatt's major alterations were undertaken (*see* Plate 2). His pen and ink sketch of 1799 shows the house after the alterations. This view shows a number of people enjoying recreation on and around the pool; figures are fishing, boating and gazing out across the water (*see* Fig. 10, p.27). In contrast the earlier view is completely empty of people. This may show changes in the way the pool was used, or may be Phillp consciously practising the depiction of people. Visitors were certainly given permission to fish in the pool at times, for example William Cheshire wrote to Doctor Solomon in 1804, 'Dr Solomon is welcome to

30   *Temple of Flora and Shell Pool, by John Phillp, c.1795.*
This shows, on either side of the Temple, the planting supplied
by Brunton and Forbes in 1787-8 and graded for height,
together with the artificial shell installed in 1778 where the
spring water ran into the pool.

take a day's fishing in Mr Boulton's pool, by way of convincing himself that it is an unprofitable way of spending his time; for where there is little in, little can be taken out.'[37] Francis Eginton junior's similar view includes livestock and swans but only two figures in the boat (*see* Fig. 11, p.27).

As well as giving details of the surroundings of the Manufactory and house, Phillp's work provides images of the various garden buildings which are described in the bills and letters and discussed in Chapters One and Two. It is Phillp's views which allow us to confirm that the buildings constructed at Soho were so strongly inspired by Boulton's visit to Painshill. However, they can be misleading: the 1794 view of the Temple of Flora (*see* Plate 3) shows a classical building in isolation with some rough grass in front of it and steps leading up to it. The image appears to suggest the temple sits on a mound. An undated pen and ink view shows it from the other side of Shell Pool and makes clear not only its proximity to the pool but also the extent to which it was surrounded by dense vegetation. Another view pulls back even further from the temple, down the

slope and to the far side of Soho Pool making even clearer the extent and density of the vegetation and the size of the estate (*see* Fig. 3, p.9). Similarly, Phillp's views of the Hermitage add to our understanding of the 'building adapted for contemplation' from which William Small's monument could be seen and provide some information on what the interior may have been like (*see* Plate 6) (though in the latter case it is unclear how much of the ornament shown in the drawing was actually in place).[38] It is also Phillp's work which confirms the entry in a bill for painting a coat of arms on a boat, and his measured drawing which shows accurately the style of the sphinxes on the walk and which, when the originals were traced, helped to identify them (*see* Figs 17 and 18). Phillp's views give an overall feeling of the estate which is not available from any other source; for instance his 'sketch in Soho' of 1801 shows the boundary between the front lawns of the house and the grazing land of the park. It was Phillp who showed that there was still a 'barren heath' and woodland around Soho in spite of the enclosures carried out in 1792 (*see* Plate 2).

A further insight into the landscape and the changes wrought on it by Boulton is provided by a poem transcribed by Phillp.[39] Created to look like loose sheets of paper it contains 'Verses on Soho […] Addressed to Matthew Boulton Esq by a friend who saw Soho when Mr B first settled there in 1775,[40] And saw it again in 1796 in its improved state'. The author of the poem is not known. Phillp notes at the bottom of the verse that it was written on separate sheets, in the same handwriting 'but by whom I could never learn', and no further information has been found. Written in Liverpool in 1796 it begins:

> *Where Nature seem'd to have left a spot for waste,*
> *And barren heath defied all human taste*
> *Where tree nor Shrub, except the furze bush grew,*
> *Became the chosen seat of Art and you*

The poet goes on to outline the way in which Boulton added plantations of firs which provided protection from the wind and 'sheltered modest science from the road.' Then he suggests the Goddess of Invention came and spread news of Boulton's genius, and how, amidst 'a Crowd of Patents', with the help of Industry, she went on to 'make fertile soil of sand' and 'plan a mansion fit for its chosen band' before returning to her cell to sketch the plan now realised by Boulton. The poet emphasises that it was industry and art that transformed this 'dreary Waste' so that it:

> *Now boasts a garden of my homely taste.*
> *Rest here – the Vista and the Shady bowers*
> *Enrich my farm encircled now with flowers:*

It rejects the influence of people like Knight, Price or Burke, but suggests that as it is not possible to please everyone, Boulton has chosen to please himself rather than adhering to fashionable theories. The poet concludes by wishing Boulton will live long to enjoy his 'well earned fame' and that,

> *Whilst science lives, none will forget your Name.*
> *May a long line of Sons enjoy a Seat,*
> *Where, Welcome All, the best skilled often met,*
> *May Genius, Virtue, Science, Wit or Art,*
> *When in the course of Nature you depart.*
> *Never desert that Mansion, to bemoan*
> *A loss for which none living can atone!*

This wish did not come true. Matthew Boulton's son, M.R. Boulton, enjoyed Soho but his grandson, M.P.W. Boulton, used the Great Tew estate bought by M.R. Boulton in 1815 as his country seat and let Soho House. Neither is Boulton's name as well remembered as the poet wished.

Boulton evidently approved of these lines but perhaps felt they could be improved upon, for he drafted two alternative versions. One of these appears in his notebook (quoted in Chapter One), and another has been added by Phillp to his transcribed verses:

> *Nor Tree nor Shrub around 'ere knew this land*
> *Till planted nurs'd & watered by my hand,*
> *By industry & art, a dreary Waste*
> *Now shews a Garden of my homely taste.*

> *Nor Knight, nor Price, nor Burk, Sublime,*
> *I will not ape in Prose or Rhime,*
> *Nor Forest make, but Garden neat,*
> *With here and there a resting seat.*
> *Formd from the dreary Waste by me,*
> *Who planted every Shrub & Tree,*
> *To skreen me from the Northern Breeze,*
> *But most of all myself to please.*

The altered wording identifies areas of particular importance to Boulton, for instance the insertion of 'watered' into the care of the trees is because he used the Manufactory steam engine to raise water to flood areas and water trees, a new technique discussed in Chapter One, the costs of which the garden designer Humphry Repton had asked him about in 1789.[41] Following the theme of the original poet, he rejected the ideas of Knight, Price and Burke, but emphasised the neatness and practicality of his garden with its resting seats and windbreaks. He reiterated the idea that it was his own work, done to please himself.

The Phillp album also contains images of Dash, the Boulton family dog, designs for the Library at Soho House, and designs for doors and surrounds which may relate to nearby Thornhill House, from December 1818 the home of Boulton's daughter, Anne. Other known Phillp material includes a portrait of the lady's maid, Martha Adcock, and a drawing of the butler polishing plate. These subjects also indicate the fact that Phillp had privileged access to family and staff. There are views of the surrounding areas including Aston Church and a 'Hut in the pleasure grounds of the Earl of Dartmouth, Sandwell' (*see* Plate 12), a building the location of which is now unknown. Some views remain unidentified. Some may be imaginary, while others may depict real places as yet unrecognised, including at Soho. Yet others are composite, for example a boat apparently belonging to Matthew Boulton[42] is shown on a lake with mountainous backdrop. The dated images we have of Soho are all from relatively early in Phillp's career, when he was probably around eighteen years old. It is not clear if he ceased to draw the Soho estate after that point, or if there were later images which have not survived or are not known. Later images would prove fascinating as it is clear he continued to develop as an artist and designer.

FOUR

THE NEXT GENERATIONS, 1809-49

Phillada Ballard and Val Loggie

Matthew Boulton had lived at Soho for 40 years by the time of his death in 1809, and it would remain the family home for a further 40 years, initially in the hands of Boulton's son, Matthew Robinson Boulton (1770-1842). It was not until 1817 that M.R. Boulton, by then aged 47, married Mary Anne Wilkinson (1795-1829). Mary Anne (or Marianne) was the daughter of William Wilkinson and niece of John 'Iron Mad' Wilkinson; she was also the niece of Joseph Priestley's wife, Mary. M.R. Boulton, and his wife went on to have seven children, six of whom survived to adulthood (Mary Anne died a few days after giving birth to their last child, also named Mary Anne).

In 1815, two years before his marriage, Matthew Robinson Boulton had bought a 3,000 acre country estate, Tew Park in Oxfordshire. M.R. Boulton and his family used Tew Park seasonally for shooting and holidays but Soho remained his base. Evidence that Soho remained the main family home for some decades comes in the form of letters and diaries written from Soho in the 1820s, 1830s and 1840s, and watercolours and sketches by two of M.R. Boulton's children, Katherine (1819-90) and Hugh Boulton (1821-47), and his sister-in-law Elizabeth Stockdale Wilkinson, which are of the Soho Estate or were done at Soho.[1] Examination of Katherine Boulton's diaries for 1841-3 show that she spent most of her time at Soho, with about two months each year at Tew, generally some time between July and October. It is, however, clear that it was mostly the women of the family who remained at Soho in the 1840s; their brothers visited regularly, but M.P.W. Boulton was at Trinity College, Cambridge, Hugh at Christ Church, Oxford, and later in the Lifeguards, and Montagu (1823-49) was also away. Soho was obviously regarded much more as home by the women, who wrote about it with great affection, later returning to visit 'old Soho'.[2]

It was not until after the mid-19th century that the Boultons finally left Soho and severed their direct connections with industry. From that time on they lived principally at Tew, and at the nearby estate of Haseley Court, whilst drawing an increasing income from urban rents in Birmingham, an expedient followed by old and new rich alike if they were the fortunate possessors of land in the vicinity of an expanding centre of population and industry. Matthew Boulton's decision to buy the freehold of Soho in 1794 had proved very beneficial for his descendants.

But while Matthew Robinson Boulton was still in charge of Soho the demesne and homestead estate remained virtually intact, although some building leases were granted on outlying portions of the estate.

M.R. Boulton had taken some interest in the gardens at Soho, especially as his father's health began to fail. However, as his father had once observed, the business at the Manufactory did not allow him much time to devote to the garden, so he was probably relatively inexperienced in estate and garden management at the time he took over responsibility for Soho in 1809. He would therefore have needed someone with the necessary expertise to run it efficiently. In 1810 he took on a new head gardener, Alexander Stephenson (or Stevenson), who came with excellent references.[3] He and his wife and children were given the gardener's cottage.

At about this time M.R. Boulton was thinking of planting an orchard, and one of Stephenson's first tasks was to go to a nursery run by James Biggs at Worcester to look at the stock. On his return to Soho, Stephenson gave his employer a good report of the fruit trees and made some suggestions, but wrote to Biggs later that in the meantime his master had received the advice that 'the removal of Fruit Trees northerly is the reverse of good Gardening, & especially to this bleak & sterile soil, from so mild & rich a spot as your Nursery'.[4] As a result he had been instructed to look for stock from nurseries in Lancashire instead. Four days later, Stephenson set out from Soho to Lancashire with letters of introduction to two nurserymen in the district, William Butler of Prescot, and a Mr Taylor of Preston.[5] He went first to see Butler's nursery, and the next day to Preston to Mr Taylor's,[6] but suffered a catastrophic accident on the mail coach taking him back from Preston to Liverpool for the night. News of the misfortune was relayed to Soho by the landlord of the *Liverpool Inn* to which the injured man was taken, and through his clerk, Zack Walker, M.R. Boulton wrote to Whitehouse and Galan, a Liverpool business house with which he had dealings, asking them to see that no expense was spared in treating the gardener. The best doctors were summoned and regular letters from Whitehouse over the next few days give a harrowing account of the gardener's suffering before his death on 22 October.[7] Arrangements were subsequently made by William Cheshire for Mrs Stephenson to receive some parochial relief; she moved to Gloucestershire and, with some help from M.R. Boulton and another of her late husband's former employers, set up a day-school and took in lodgers to enable her to support her family. Her eldest boy, John, was taken on at the Soho Manufactory to work in the plate company, where his behaviour and aptitude met with approval, so that M.R. Boulton paid for him to go to school and occasionally invited him to eat at Soho House.[8]

Following this tragic episode it seems to have been 1811 before M.R. Boulton was able to really focus his attention again on the Soho orchard, and he once more sought advice. In 1812 James Watt junior sent a list of fruit trees in the orchards at Heathfield[9] and judging by the correlation of ticks on this list and the varieties ordered that autumn, Watt's advice was followed.[10] There were two orchards at Soho. One was on the land below the canal and the area of the old kitchen garden and was probably the continuation of an orchard started by Matthew Boulton. It occupied an area 160 yards (146.30 metres) by 32 yards (29.26 metres) and had 140 trees planted quincuncially (that is, arranged in groups of five, like the five on a dice)[11] and the other was in front of the new kitchen garden (*see* Fig. 32).[12] The characteristics and progress of the fruit trees was recorded by the new gardener, P. Beahan, in a large notebook entitled *Pomona Sohoniensis 1811-1821*.[13] William Butler at Prescot also supplied information on the planting and care of the fruit trees (*see* Fig. 33), as follows:

> Mr Butlers method of Planting Fruit Trees is to take out a Trench or Hole the depth of the natural Soil and by no means <u>any deeper</u> then to lay a coat of Marl 4 feet wide, and as long as convenient; the marl to be not less than 4 Inches – Should the natural depth of the soil be more than 2 feet 6 inches, He would not go deeper with his Coat of Marl contending that even good Soil placed below that depth, becomes in a short time crude and unfit for Vegetable purposes. There are many reasons to be adduced

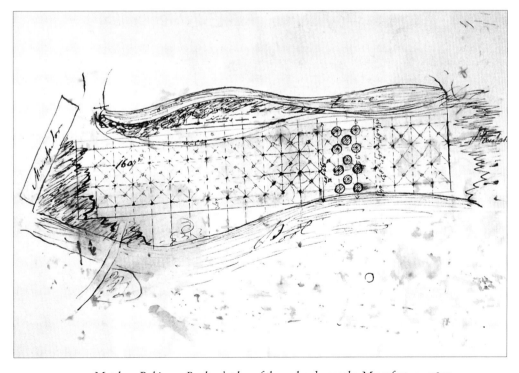

31 *Matthew Robinson Boulton's plan of the orchard near the Manufactory, 1812.*

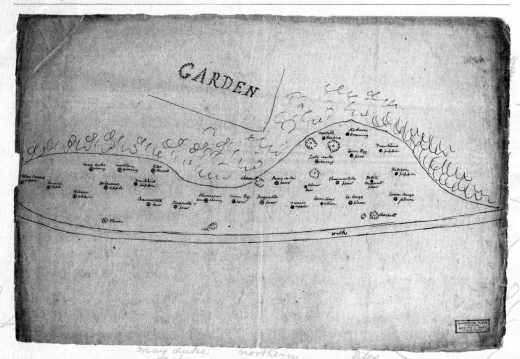

32   *Plan of the orchard by the new kitchen garden c.1815.*

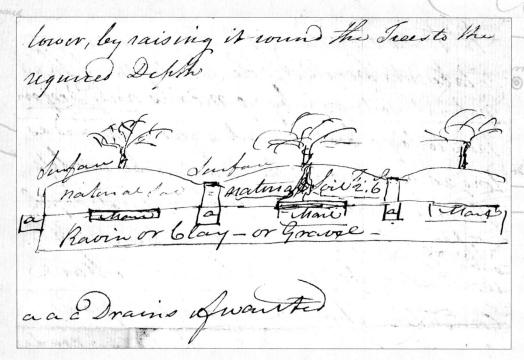

33   'Mr Butler's method of Planting Fruit Trees' – sketch from an undated memorandum of advice from William Butler, a nurseryman at Prescot, Lancashire, who supplied Matthew Robinson Boulton with trees for his orchard in 1812.

against going deeper, the most material of which is it encourages the Root to go lower down than it can find food in a Horrizontal way further than the preparation, and it is not natural for a Root to go upwards. He would rather advise raising the Soil higher than going lower, by raising it round the Trees to the required depth.[14]

Further details were noted around the same time in another memorandum headed 'Orders to be given to the Gardener for the proper management and pruning of the new planted trees':

1. Towards the end of March or the beginning of April according to the forwardness or backwardness of the season, when the buds begin to shoot, head the trees to five eyes if the shoots are weak and to six, seven or eight according their strength, observing to cut them sloping on the wall's side and as near the top buds as may be, and also to rub off the foresight shoots.
2. Never fail to rub on a little of the following composition where you cut off the top of the shoots and don't nail them to the wall until they are grown so long and strong as to be exposed to be broken by the wind.
   Composition:
   Take two quarts of fresh cow-dung, one quart of lime rubbish of old building, and one quart of wood ashes, both sifted fine, add to it a handful of pit or river sand, mix the whole and work it together with a wooden beater until the stuff is very smooth like fine plaster used for the ceilings, and you will have it so by adding a sufficient quantity of soap-suds.[15]

The trees on the various lists, which included named varieties of pears, apples, peaches, cherries, plums, filberts and nuts, were chosen for cropping at different seasons and some for their keeping qualities. Some 14 pear varieties included Jargonelle, Little Muscat, Summer Bergamot and Black Worcester, some of them to be dwarfs grafted onto quince stocks. There were Early May and Kensington Duke cherries, and Baxters Pearmain, Yorkshire Greening, French Crab, and Franklins Pippin among 15 varieties of apples 'For keeping & kitchen Fruit'.[16] The fruit trees evidently established well, for cuttings from the Soho orchards were sent to Great Tew when an orchard was being established there in 1819.[17]

M.R. Boulton also sought advice on flowering shrubs and herbaceous material. His cousin George Mynd was consulted and his 'List of flower-roots etc. proper for Soho' dated November 1812[18] appears to have been largely followed, judging by the surviving orders to nursery firms in 1813. In fact in this year there was a very considerable purchase of new shrubs and herbaceous plants, suggesting that either existing borders needed restocking, or that new borders were being established. An order to the famous Hammersmith nursery of Lee and Kennedy included several rhododendrons, azaleas, magnolias and andromeda. The four rhododendrons were two species which had long been in cultivation, *R. hirsutum* and *R. ferrugineum*, originally introduced from Europe, and two very recent introductions from eastern North America, *R. catawbiense* and *R. roseum*. The azaleas included 'Azalea viscosa praecox', now *R.viscosa*, also from eastern North America but introduced in 1734, and three now unidentifiable varieties named A. floribunda, A. orange, and A. scarlet. The two magnolias were *M. tripetala* introduced from Eastern North America in 1752 and *M. liliflora* from Central China introduced in 1790. Many of the 51 varieties of roses are now impossible to identify, but the order did include one very recent introduction, the Fairy Rose, *R. Lawranceana*, which had first been on sale at Colville's nursery in 1805.[19] The bill for the total of 245 varieties of flowering shrubs came to £37 11s. 6d.[20] There were also several orders for bulbs and flower seeds, including one to Gordon, Forsyth & Co., the London firm from whom Matthew Boulton had often ordered seeds.[21] M.R. Boulton seems to have shared his father's and his sister's love of flowers, for a list survives of 77 different types of 'flower seeds sowed in the garden and pleasure ground at Soho 1813' and over 90 biennials and perennials 'planted in flower beds and border by Mr Beahan, 1813'.[22] Many must have been used along the Sphinx Walk, which led from the house to the gardener's cottage and which a contemporary recalled as being 'very pretty, a combination of flower beds on each side.'[23]

With the new planting becoming established, in June 1814 the public had a chance to see the grounds when they were admitted to Soho for the premature celebrations of peace in the war with France. As in 1802, the Manufactory was illuminated, but this time not the house. Although there was a crowd of 50,000 people, Matthew Robinson Boulton noted that 'His park has suffered less injury from the great pressure than he had

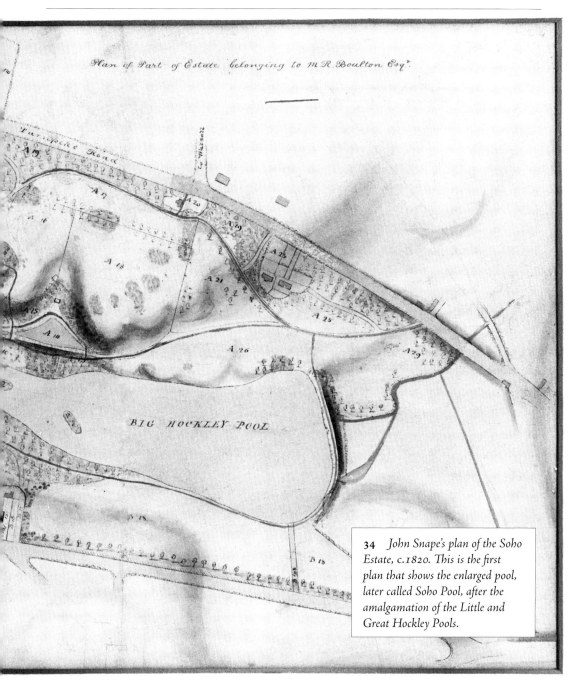

34 *John Snape's plan of the Soho Estate, c.1820. This is the first plan that shows the enlarged pool, later called Soho Pool, after the amalgamation of the Little and Great Hockley Pools.*

reason to expect, so careful were the visitors not to abuse that liberality which was so freely exercised for their gratification.'[24]

In later years there were many orders for bulbs, together with new vogue plants such as dahlias, four roots of which were ordered from Lee and Kennedy in 1818.

These were not successfully grown in Britain before 1804, when Lady Holland procured some plants. Boulton's order came with detailed instructions:

> The Dahlia roots we pot now and put them in gentle heat and afterwards set them in the greenhouse till end of May when the frost being over we turn them out of pots where they are to flower they naturally flower late[,] by this mode we get them two months earlier in flower.[25]

Another novelty was to construct rockeries, and Boulton ordered 'plants for rockwork' from J. Moore in 1820.[26] In the 1830s some of the flower beds were edged with metalwork baskets.[27]

Two changes to the Soho landscaping are shown on maps of the 1820s. Snape's Plan of *c*.1820 (*see* Fig. 34) indicates that the causeway dam between the two sections of the Hockley Pool had been removed, making one large lake, and the promontory had become another island. The Pigott Smith map of 1828 shows that the kitchen garden had been laid out in its final rectangular form. The garden was watered from a system of 17 underground tanks which were fed from a spring, and it is known that these were installed by 1823. In the following year Boulton brought an action against the Wednesbury and Birmingham Turnpike Trust who had improved the Soho road by reducing the gradient, as part of Thomas Telford's upgrading of the Holyhead to London route. Boulton claimed that the accesses to his estate had been blocked and had had to be remade, the spring to the tanks had been blocked off, and the estate's potential for building had been reduced. However, Boulton lost his action.[28]

It has been suggested that after Mrs Mary Anne Boulton's death in 1829 her husband took less interest in the gardens and that their beauties waned,[29] but this may have been temporary. A new greenhouse was bought in 1830 and M.R. Boulton's daughter, Katherine Elizabeth Boulton, wrote to her sister, Anne Robinson Boulton (1818-1902, known by the family as Diddle), in October that year adding that 'I think you will be pleased with the new Greenhouse, it is coming on very fast and I hope will be built by the time you return'.[30] The location of the greenhouse is undocumented, but it may have been built as a wall house in the kitchen garden, and an undated sketch has survived which shows such a structure with thin metal glazing bars, though this may be for a later glasshouse erected in 1840.[31] These metallic hothouses were very fashionable, though expensive, and they enabled more light reach the interior. They had been manufactured in

35 *Soho Estate section from J. Piggott Smith's* Map of Birmingham, *1828. The kitchen garden with its four rectangular beds can be seen alongside the turnpike road.*

Birmingham since 1818. The greenhouse was at some distance from the house but walking to it provided exercise and enjoyment for the Misses Boulton, and they were frequently joined by their friends who had called on them, as on 24 June 1842 when Katherine noted in her diary 'the 2 Miss Barkers came and Miss Corrie and we all went to the greenhouse to look at the Ipomea.'[32]

Katherine Boulton's diaries also record visits in the Spring by her father, Miss Wilkinson or her sisters to local nurseries, among them More's, Pope's, Dickenson's and Miss Whitmore's. A new garden was being planned in 1843 and Katherine wrote to her brother, Matthew Piers Watt Boulton:

> The two poplar trees which perhaps you may remember I pointed out one day as we walked round the pool have been cut down, as during the late high winds they endangered the bank, from the proceeds of the same will come the posts and rails for the new garden.[33]

Other evidence would also suggest that the gardens, 40 acres of pools, park and plantations were in a thriving condition with repairs being done to 'the garden house', probably the Temple, in 1836, and the grotto house in 1833,[34] and the boat house.[35] The pools and watercourses were kept in repair and remudded where necessary, the greatest expenditure being £279 to repair Big Hockley Pool dam in 1811 after floods.[36] Extensive work was also carried out at Shell Pool in 1837 to stop it leaking, and the walks around it were re-gravelled in 1840.[37] It was of course vital for the industrial processes at the Manufactory that the pools and waterways were kept in good order.

Among the family's enjoyments at Soho were hot air ballooning,[38] boating and fishing.

M.R. Boulton also continued to run the homestead farm, which varied between 29 and 45 acres, and he ran a stud at Soho. The Soho desmene was run by a head gardener with a staff of six who worked six days a week.[39] M.R. Boulton extended the area of workmen's gardens established by his father, doubling those near the Manufactory to 45 gardens which covered an area of over six acres.[40] In 1822 he laid out a further 32 guinea gardens on the Slade for his workmen, which comprised seven acres, and was the area south of the mill pool.[41]

Some building leases were granted on the Soho estate in the areas designated by his father, that is, adjoining the turnpike road and along the Nineveh Road, for small houses in small plots.[42] By 1821 there were 30 leases, and 48 by 1843. The land which Matthew Boulton had improved as farmland after he purchased it, continued to be let as such. However, the potential of the Soho demesne for building was an important consideration although as yet unrealised. In 1833 large quantities of timber were felled in an area of the park 'lying on a piece of land near to Soho Turnpike' and sold at auction.[43] This was generally a prelude to land being let for building, but it did not happen immediately so perhaps the time was not yet thought to be right.

PLATE 1 *Carl Frederick von Breda:* Matthew Boulton, *1792. Von Breda's portrait shows Boulton holding a medal and a magnifying glass. There are mineral specimens on the table beside him, and the Soho Manufactory is visible in the*

PLATE 2 *John Phillp's 1796 view of the Soho estate from Birmingham Heath illustrates the unpromising vegetation that prevailed at Soho before Matthew Boulton carried out his improvements to the 'barren waste' of the former Handsworth Heath where Soho was situated. At the far right a team of horses can be seen pulling a waggon bearing an engine cylinder.*

PLATE 3 *Watercolour of the Temple of Flora by John Phillp, 1794. In this view Phillp concentrates on the architectural details of the building including the green shutters to exclude the elements.*

PLATE 4 *John Phillp's 1795 watercolour of the Little Hockley Pool which Boulton had made in 1775 to increase the water for the Manufactory, but which was also an ornamental feature. The peninsula below the Manufactory, created at the same time, was used by Boulton for his kitchen garden which was partly enclosed by a fruit wall.*

PLATE 5   *The Hermitage in snow, by John Phillp, c.1795. This building was erected in 1775 in a clearing made in the woodland planted in the early 1760s.*

PLATE 6   *The interior view of the Hermitage contrasted with the rustic exterior, John Phillp, 1799.*

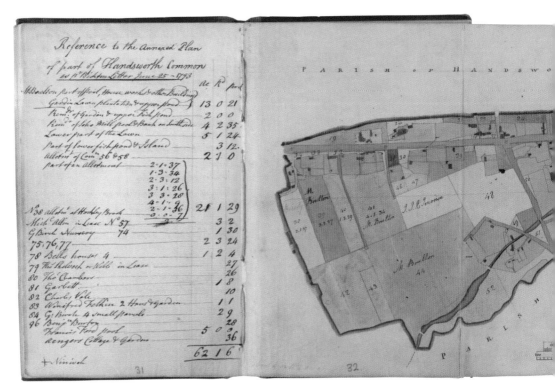

PLATE 7 *Section from Matthew Boulton's plan of his landholdings (coloured green) at Soho of 1793, showing his planned extensions to the existing walks on the additional land purchased in 1794-5.*

PLATE 8 *View of the path to the Soho Manufactory from the latchet works, by an unknown artist. This is the only known image of the building from this direction, and echoes Boulton's own idea in a notebook to 'make all entrances in to Soho Dark by Plantations and enter through Gothick arches made by trees' (see Chapter Two).*

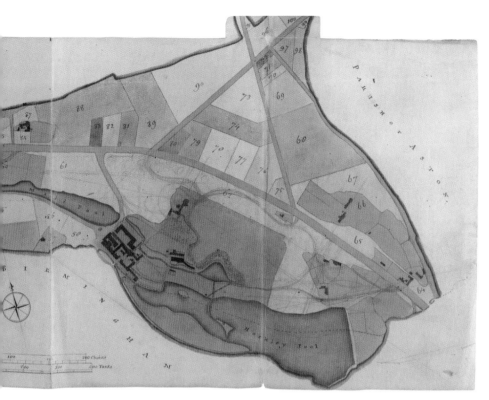

PLATE 9 *Interior of a garden building with views from its windows, by John Phillp, 1799. This is probably a composite drawing with views placed in the windows of an imaginary building. The left-hand window shows a view of the Temple of Flora and Shell Pool and the right-hand view may be the rear of the Manufactory or a view of buildings on the Soho turnpike. The building may have some resemblance to the 'wooden building' that was placed near Shell Pool in 1794.*

PLATE 10 *Elevation of the boathouse entrance, by John Phillp, c.1801.*
This may have been a design for the boathouse erected at the far end of Great
Hockley Pool in 1801.

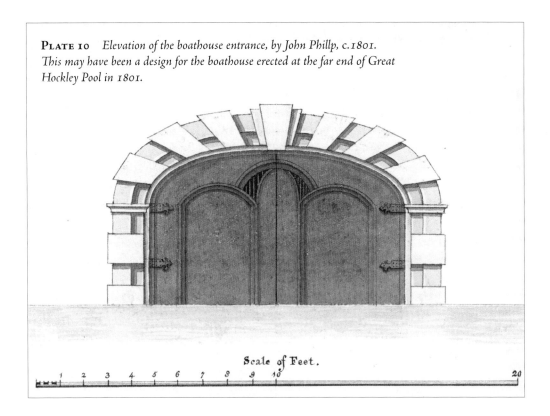

Scale of Feet.

PLATE 11   *View of an ornamental vase on a pediment placed beneath a tree on an eminence at the rear*
of Soho House, by John Phillp, 1799. Part of the elevation of the principal building of the Manufactory also
appears in this drawing, indicating the steepness of the slope leading to it from Boulton's house. The white
house in the distance (far right) is Thornhill House, the home of Miss Anne Boulton from 1818-29.

PLATE 12 *Hut in the pleasure grounds of the Earl of Dartmouth, Sandwell, watercolour by John Phillp, 1807.*

PLATE 13 *Watercolour of Soho Pool by Alan Everitt, c.1855. This view shows the pool towards the north.*

PLATE 14   *Soho House in April 2009.*

PLATE 15   *The reconstructed hermitage in the garden of Soho House, April 2009.*

PLATE 16   *The last organic fragment of Matthew Boulton's garden: the lid of this small (unhallmarked) silver-mounted box is inscribed inside, 'ZW Lid from an old oak in the grounds at Soho'. ZW was either Matthew Boulton's brother-in-law Zaccheus Walker senior (d.1808) or his nephew Zaccheus Walker junior (1768-1822). Base approximately 10.2 x 7.4 cm, height 4cm. (Private Collection.)*

Matthew Robinson Boulton made a few further purchases of land, mainly small amounts which his father had previously leased. He died at Soho on 18 April 1842, and the estate then passed to his eldest son, Matthew Piers Watt Boulton. In 1843, at the time of the Handsworth Tithe Assessment, M.P.W. Boulton owned 134 acres plus a further eight acres of land leased for building, and at the Birmingham Tithe of 1847 he was returned as owning 69 acres, making 211 acres in total. However, almost 100 acres must have been added subsequently as in 1874 the Boultons were described as owning 300 acres.[44]

M.P.W. Boulton evidently regarded Great Tew as his base; he seems to have had little emotional attachment to Soho and was less involved in the businesses there; under his stewardship the process of capitalising on the estate began in earnest.

In 1845 he married Frances Eliza Cartwright of Aynhoe Park (an estate about six miles south-east of Banbury, over the county boundary in Northamptonshire), and held a feast for 400 people at Tew.[45] Two years later he purchased the Great Milton estate near to Tew, for £185,000. This comprised 3,900 acres and included an 18th-century mansion, Haseley Court,[46] which became the residence of his sister, Katherine, who in January 1844 had married James Patrick Muirhead at Handsworth Chapel (Handsworth Parish Church, St Mary's).[47] The Boultons now had an established county position based on broad acres. In 1847-8 there is evidence for items of furniture, books, silverware and other household goods being moved from Soho to Tew by boat.[48] This seems to have been a prelude to the breaking up of the Soho Estate, which M.P.W. Boulton began to do from 1849.

Up till that time, shortly before the Boulton family left Soho for good, the grounds were essentially still intact, and the public was afforded a glimpse of the house, gardens and park when, in conjunction with the Handsworth and Lozells Horticultural Exhibition, held in the grounds of Hockley Abbey, access was again allowed into Soho Park, where 'its noble sheet of water and the pleasant walks afforded much gratification to a very numerous company'.[49] An eyewitness account of the occasion, though not published until 1911, gives a rare description of a walk through the grounds of Soho before it was developed:

> The visitors to the flower show were, however, privileged to pass across the little bridge and floodgate along the dam of the great pool, by the winding walks among the trees to the Shell Pool, which lay hidden half-way up the hillside. This was a retired spot of remarkable beauty – on the upper side was a well designed but somewhat dilapidated summer house, its site sloping to the water's edge. The water was dark from the overhanging boughs of the thickly-growing trees, and the surrounding paths were overhung with varied foliage. From Shell Pool the walk passed the buildings of the still famous Mint, erected in 1788, and onwards past the extensive stables diverging upwards to Soho House on the higher ground and to the Soho Factory on the lower. These diverging pathways were numerous and intricate, the lower ones extended over somewhat marshy ground at the extreme end of the great pool and onward to the Nineveh side, where extensions had been made by Mr Boulton upon

the enclosure of the Handsworth and Birmingham common lands. It was, however, the upper paths which led to the point of chief interest, Soho House …

The same writer emphasised the total seclusion of the park, a measure of how successfully Matthew Boulton had

shut out the sights of the world, so that the estate had been hidden behind a formidable split oak fence which surmounted a low brick wall, and from Hockley Brook to Factory Road the thick foliage of the well-wooded domain effectually obstructed the view, even of the outside passenger by the passing coach. The monotony of this fence had for many years been varied only by a quaint iron pump, a massive milestone, the park lodge, and the turnpike gate. Now, however, the barrier was pierced and 'intended roads' aroused the attention of architect and builder to that section of the park fronting Soho Hill.[50]

Those 'intended roads' signalled that this seclusion was soon to end.

FIVE

THE CHANGING SCENE AT SOHO:
BUILDING ESTATE AND INDUSTRIAL USE, 1850-1990

Phillada Ballard and Val Loggie

Matthew Piers Watt Boulton had clearly given much thought to the Boulton family's future at Soho and the potential of the estate. In 1846, three years before the closing of the Manufactory and his initial withdrawal from the business, he had granted the first of 15 building leases on the one-acre Stoney Field, formerly part of the Soho Homestead farm.[1] The first part of the main Soho estate to be developed was in 1849. This was the area furthest from the house near Hockley Bridge by the turnpike, including the kitchen garden. Here two new roads, Richmond Road and Claremont Road, were built to form a triangle and leases were granted for small plots.[2] However, instead of continuing with piecemeal development of this type, M.P.W. Boulton decided on a masterplan for the development of the whole of the Soho demesne, which was called Soho Park. It is evident from numerous surviving rough outline plans of different parts of the estate that the plan produced was very much his concept.[3]

M.P.W. Boulton had by this time left from Soho House and was considering letting it. The Honourable Lieutenant Colonel Scarlett, commanding the regiment then stationed at Birmingham Barracks, and a Frederick Giles of the Oaklands, Handsworth, both expressed an interest in taking the house for a short time but Boulton appeared to have had second thoughts, as he left instructions that no one else was to be shown the house. Boulton's agent, Chubb, argued that letting the house would be advantageous, presumably as it would prevent it falling into disrepair, but possibly also because there were rumours that Boulton had overstretched himself financially when purchasing the Haseley Estate.[4] In spite of this, Boulton continued to delay and it was not until June 1850 that work began to clear the house of family possessions.[5] This was largely complete by November and the house was to be advertised to let.[6] The house was listed as unoccupied in the *Post Office Directory of Birmingham, 1851*.

Having moved what he wanted from Soho to Tew, in 1851, M.P.W. Boulton at last advertised Soho House to let in *Aris's Birmingham Gazette* and the *Midland*

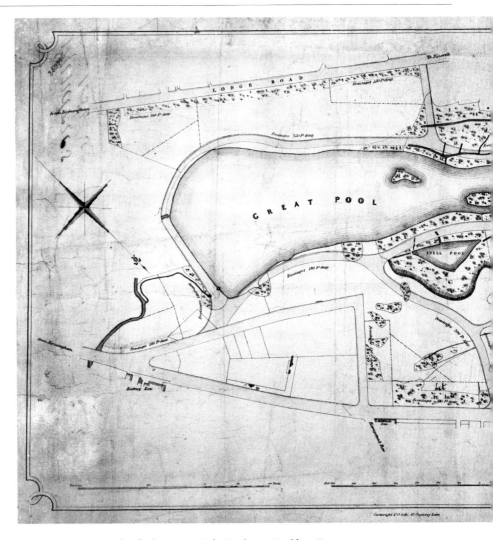

36 *Plan for laying out Soho Park as a Building Estate, c.1853.*

Counties Herald, without success. In June 1852 it was advertised again, and finally on 29 September that year Alfred Toy, a lamp manufacturer, took it on a 14-year lease.[7] Toy also leased parts of the Manufactory and 'the Shell Pool Pleasure grounds' on a yearly tenancy at £20 'subject to a months notice to quit if required for building'.[8] Notwithstanding these leases, Toy had presumably left by October 1858, when the house was advertised again in *Aris's Gazette*. That was also the year in which the Soho Manufactory was finally closed by M.P.W. Boulton, reacting to the demands of the residents of the new villas, who objected to the noise and smoke of a working manufactory nearby. The Manufactory's tenant businesses (the old Boulton family businesses having by now all been sold off or closed down) were moved to a new site at Spring Hill, and M.P.W. Boulton briefly contemplated converting the

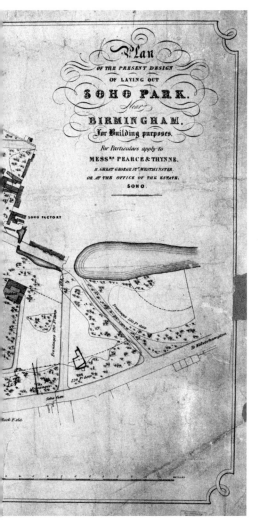

Manufactory Principal Building into 'four first-rate dwellings' before deciding it should be demolished, which was done over the next few years.[9] If the conversion proposal had been carried out, the Soho Manufactory might well still be standing.

The development of the Soho Park building estate, which comprised most of the land of the private gardens and park of Soho House, differed from that of the other land of the Boulton estate, at least in its initial phases, in that it was for middle-class villas in a park-like setting retaining some of Matthew Boulton's landscape features. This approach was not sustained after the 1880s, when Soho House ceased to be a private house and passed into institutional use, and further industrial development in the area of Soho Pool mitigated against the continuation of detached villa development.

The 'Plan of the present design of laying out Soho Park near Birmingham for Building Purposes' had been published in 1853.[10] The design was for low-density middle-class housing with curving roads and deep frontages ranging from 150-250 feet. The pools were to be retained as attractive landscape features – the Great Pool had a planned road round its edge, making it possible to drive all round it. Shell Pool and its plantation would not be built on, and potential houses on other parts of the estate would have views of the mill pool. The Manufactory, which at that stage was still in use for industrial purposes, was shown only minimally. Soho House was to remain with its detached stables, lodge cottage, lengthy carriage drives and a still substantial garden, making it a first-rate residence and one which would add tone to the estate.

The quality of the early housing built on the estate was determined by covenants. In one agreement of 1867 with James Wilson, the builder who was responsible for many of the Soho Park houses on Soho Hill and Park Avenue, he was required to spend at least £12,000 building 'thirty good and substantial brick-built dwelling houses, such proposed erections, with fence, walls, drains etc. to be first approved of

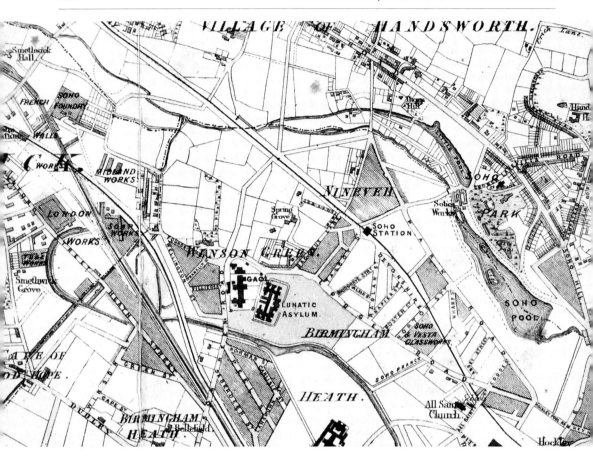

37   *Section from* Map of Birmingham and its Environs *by C.M. Blood, 1857. Part of the Hockley area of Birmingham can be seen on the far right.*

by the said Matthew Piers Watt Boulton or his agent.'[11] This price of at least £400 per house was exceeded by the £600 for each house specified in an agreement with John Skidmore for two houses on Soho Hill.[12] A map of Birmingham and outlying parishes in 1857 by Henry Blood[13] clearly shows how the development of the estate had proceeded, with the earliest part in the triangle of roads densely built on, and large villa residences along Soho Hill up to the mill pool and a short way into the estate along Park Avenue. No building had taken place on the other side of the Great Pool, perhaps because the several roads of terraced housing leading off Lodge Road were a deterrent. James Muirhead (a descendant and biographer of James Watt, who married Katherine Elizabeth Boulton) saw the estate at this point:

> The 'sepulchred grove' of Soho has fallen; the 'sarcophagus', or rather cenotaph – has perished; and the romantic grounds surrounding Mr Boulton's mansion with their woods and waters, little more than a century ago an unpeopled and uncultured waste, then transformed into a series of smiling gardens and shaded lawns, have

now become the site of other houses, multiplying in proportion to the immense development of the steam-engine and its results in that central and busy district of our great manufacturing country.[14]

However, from early on the layout of the development near Soho House did not proceed as in the published plan, for in 1853 St Michael's Church was built on land immediately to the north of the house, with an additional road, Soho Avenue, being made between the house and the church. This was the second new church to be built in Handsworth as the result of the rapidly increasing population and was built on land purchased from the Boulton Trustees for £300. The church was designed by W. Bourne of Dudley. It was recorded that when the church was built 'there were yet some remains of Handsworth Heath and the rude paths across it. The woods of Soho Park sloped gently to the lake below.'[15]

The vicar of the newly constructed Church, Rev. George Boyle, was the next tenant of Soho House at about the time the demolition of the Soho Manufactory started. He visited the house in June 1860 and agreed to take it from 1 August at £120 per annum, subject to certain alterations and some major repairs and refurbishment being carried out, and subject to his mother's agreement. The specification, memorandum and estimate for the alterations show that the western end of the house was demolished at this time.[16] This was part of the wing which the Wyatts had constructed for Matthew Boulton in the 1790s and comprised the brewhouse, servant's hall, housekeeper's store, billiard room and library. The first photograph of Soho House was taken in 1863 during Boyle's tenancy. In 1860, the same year that Boyle came to Soho House, the lodge cottage was demolished and its site used for another villa, so great was the demand for sites along Soho Hill. The carriage drive to Soho House was altered to start a little way into Soho Avenue, as is shown on the plan accompanying the Rev. Boyle's agreement.

The maintenance of the estate was supervised from the 1850s by M.P.W. Boulton's agent, Edward Price. He employed day labourers, who were responsible for the undeveloped part of the estate and the immediate grounds of Soho House when it was unlet.[17] Mowing, mending fences, and repairing the pool dams were among their duties, with extra men employed for cutting down trees prior to building. When the Rev. Boyle leased Soho House, in addition to having the stables reduced in size,

38 *Photograph of Soho House in 1863, before the patent slate roof was replaced.*

he asked for the walks to be gravelled[18] and the entrance gates to be 'painted and grained',[19] indicating that the maintenance was fairly minimal.

Rev. Boyle may have left Soho House before 1868, when J. Wilson and Son were paid £410 15s. 1d. for work to the roof. He had certainly left by 29 September 1869, when the estate managers, Thynne & Thynne of Westminster, recorded that, as the house was now empty, part of the stables had been let to James Wilson (the same builder who had erected the first new houses on the estate) on a temporary basis from this date. The house was again advertised to let from 1869 to 1872, and on 25 March 1872 Wilson took it for seven years at £120 per annum, with an agreement to undertake all the repairs himself.

A letter from Katherine Elizabeth Muirhead (the Katherine Elizabeth Boulton mentioned previously) to her daughter, Beatrix, in 1880 or 1881, describes a return visit to Soho when the Wilsons were in occupation:

> Haseley Court, July 28
> My dearest Bx,
> We came home on Monday stopping for some hours en route that Papa might inspect the Watt Chapel at Handsworth. There I got him to go with me to old Soho. I enquired the name of the present occupants of the house & sent in a request to be allowed to go in, telling them who I was. A kind old lady (Mrs Wilson) at once acceded to this & begged me to go over what room I liked. They are very proud of the place and keep it in beautiful order. Some nice old pieces of Chippendale mahogany furniture left as a fixture are particularly prized and the old mahogany doors were so highly polished you would see y[ou]r face in them. Then we were introduced to the husband, a kind old man who offered to take me upstairs (as his wife was too lame). The top storey of the house is uninhabited as it is too large for their occupation but all in good order.[20]

Mr and Mrs Wilson clearly also maintained the garden to a high standard as is evident in a photograph of Soho House taken during their tenancy in *c*.1889. The fashion for bedding out and the planting of a novelty conifer, the monkey puzzle tree (*Araucaria araucana*) from Chile are contemporary notes. Also evident is the pair of lamp pedestals that were erected for Matthew Boulton by William Hollins in 1795. The Wilsons appear in Thynne & Thynne's records until the surviving accounts end in 1888. At that time Wilson was still carrying out building work on the estate for M.P.W. Boulton, laying out the Shell Pool grounds.

The availability of such a large area of parkland for development in close proximity to the rapidly expanding town attracted the attention of Birmingham Town Council, then in the process of considering for the first time the provision of public parks. An enquiry about land at Soho for a park as early as 1853 had elicited the reply that Mr Boulton had no power to sell the land and would only grant a long lease if some building was put on the ground. However, 'Mr Boulton is anxious to assist in any way he can with the improvement of the working classes

39   *Photograph of Soho House showing a star-shaped flower bed in the lawn, c.1889.*

in Birmingham.'[21] The negotiations were dropped and the Council continued with its considerations of Sutton Park and Aston Hall Park; the latter became Birmingham's first publicly-owned park in 1864.

There is some evidence that M. P. W. Boulton himself had considered developing the Great Pool for public recreation, for among his plans for cutting up the estate is a sketch of a rustic cottage 'to front the Pool'.[22] However, in 1852 he agreed a seven-year lease of the Soho Pool for public recreation to John Abrahams at an annual rent of £40.[23] The lease had the following conditions:

> To keep the fences next the Pool, the Floodgate, and the Pool dam in good order and repair.
> To have no person to fish in the Pool or to be upon the grounds unless well behaved.
> To allow no games or amusements which might be deemed an annoyance or a nuisance to the residents of the Park.
> To have the right of fishing, for himself, his friends, and subscribers, but not to use any net or nets, save the landing net.
> To have the right of road to the Pool from the Park entrance on the Staffordshire side.
> Not to remove, cut down or damage any Tree, shrub or plant that may be growing on or near the banks of the Pool.
> M.P.W. Boulton esq or his agent to have the right of granting permission for the residents of the Park to fish to the extent of twenty persons, these persons to angle only, and to have not more than one Boat amongst them, but they shall be at liberty to make any private arrangement they may think proper with Mr Abraham for the use of his boats or for fishing in any other way.

40   Sketch of Soho Pool looking southwards towards Birmingham, Samuel Lines, 1852.

41   Lithograph entitled 'Soho Lake, Soho Park, as it is at present 1854', by James Corder, showing a busy scene with many different kinds of boats, ranging from skiffs and sailing boats to a gondola and a small steamboat.

Three views of Soho Pool survive from this period: Samuel Lines's sketch of the pool and the view southwards towards Birmingham in 1852, the year that the pool was opened to the public; Alan Everitt's watercolour of the pool looking northwards of *c.*1855; the latter is more detailed and shows the maturity of the planting (*see* Plate 13); and James Corder's lithograph of 1854. The pool was occasionally used for charitable purposes. A regatta took place on the pool in 1857 for the benefit of the Blue Coat School, the races being followed by a firework display.[24]

By the 1860s the Great Pool had been leased to John Knibb and he continued it as a pleasure pool open to the public, offering 'boating, fishing, gymnasium and skating in season', and boat and fishing punt hire; the facilities of an ice-house which he had built were also

42 *Poster advertising John Knibb's boats for hire on Soho Pool, 1856.*

available. Knibb's advertisement in the 1868 *Corporation Directory for Birmingham* stated that the 'lake of twenty acres ... is beautifully situated amidst woodland and undulating scenery, and is the most pleasant retreat for a day's holiday, or an hour's rowing within 20 miles of Birmingham.' In November 1864 the lifeboat *Birmingham*, the gift of 'the working classes of the town' to the National Lifeboat Institution, was first launched on the pool.[25]

Not for much longer, however, would the people of Birmingham be able to enjoy Soho Pool. An advertisement for the Pool in *Kelly's Directory of Staffordshire* in 1868 repeated the description of the attractive scenery but added, 'Soho Lake is about to be drained, and the land appropriated for building.' Benjamin Stone photographed the pool in 1868 shortly before it was drained. The draining took eight days and cost £826. Mr Knibb was paid £30 compensation 'upon his giving up possession'.[26]

Why the decision was made to curtail Knibb's lease and drain the pool is not known. Perhaps it was felt that the crowds who went there were too rowdy and too numerous, and that in consequence builders were being deterred from taking leases near it. No builders were forthcoming however for the site of the pool, and in 1875 the Council made their second and last approach for land for a public park at Soho, the negotiations being led by the mayor, Joseph Chamberlain. He initially asked for 30 acres, subsequently reduced to 15, including the site of the

43   *Photograph by Benjamin Stone of boating scene at Soho Pool, 1868.*

pool. Like the previous application, this too was rejected, the agents Thynne & Thynne replying that M.P.W. Boulton was not willing to consider the proposal as the site under consideration was too small and 'the builders who have applied for land surrounding the site of the old pool are very averse to the project. Indeed we have concluded a negotiation with one for three acres under the assurance the park would not be formed.'[27]

There was some building of terraced housing along Park Road (the road running from St Chrysostom's Church parallel with Radnor Street on the left of the map opposite), but these were very small plots, quite different from the frontages designated on the 1852 master plan. The builders of these houses do not appear to have bid for areas of the pool site, and from 1882 the Council was availing itself of part of the site, not as a park but as a public tip.[28] In June 1883 huge public demonstrations were held on the site in support of the Franchise Bill, it being the nearest large piece of open ground to Birmingham. As a newspaper account put it, this was 'the last occasion the public had an opportunity of making use of it. Since then it has been converted into a huge coal depot, and nothing but the name seems to remind us of its former beauty.'[29] Prior to the sale of the site of the pool to the London and North Western Railway Company, James Wilson, the

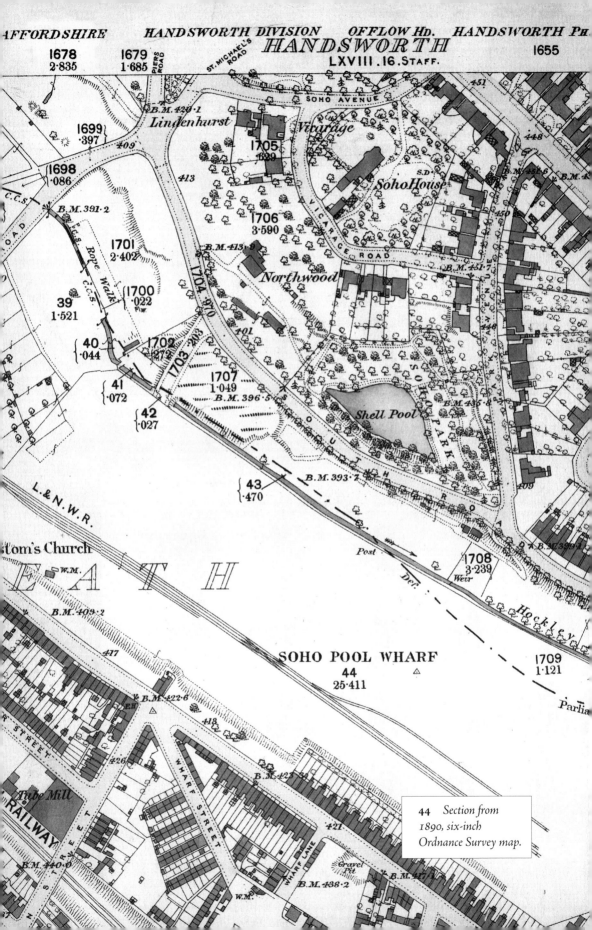

44 Section from
1890, six-inch
Ordnance Survey map.

builder of many of the Soho Park villas, sought compensation from the estate if the sale to the railway company went ahead, as it would 'depreciate the value of the houses built by him'.[30] He was awarded £4,000 compensation, and the sale of 50 acres to the railway company was concluded.

If the actual development of half of the Soho Park estate was very different from the original proposals, the progress of the areas nearer Soho House was, for a time, closer to the original plan. In 1880 the Boulton trustees laid out, at considerable expense, the Shell Pool grounds, reforming the pool, re-planting, making new walks and building a rustic bridge. This was a semi-public garden, open to subscribers only. Presumably most of these subscribers would have been residents of the nearby villas, the names of which (for example 'Northwood', 'Woodleigh', 'Woodville', 'Oak Bank', and 'Beechwood') reflected their attractively wooded gardens, the surviving remnants of Matthew Boulton's original plantings. The grounds near Soho House remained essentially the same, apart from the loss of the lodge, until in 1871, when the house was untenanted, the stables were demolished.[31] A new road, Vicarage Road, was built, cutting through the site of the stables and encircling the house, and a new stable and courtyard were added to the house with an exit onto Vicarage Road.[32] The gardens immediate to the house retained much of their original planting.

45 *Photograph of the Shell Pool Grounds c.1880. The Temple of Flora once stood on the slope just abov the pool.*

46   *Photograph of two of the subscribers to the Shell Pool grounds on the bridge across the overspill to Soho Pool.*

The Wilsons had left by 1893 when the house was in use for some years as a girls' school. Photographs in the Stone Collection at Birmingham Central Library show Mrs and Miss Taylor and some of their pupils standing outside the house, and Kelly's *Directory of Birmingham* for 1896 lists a Ladies' School under Miss Janet Harriet Taylor.

Matthew Piers Watt Boulton died in 1894 and the estate passed to his son, Matthew Ernest Boulton. In that year a developer, Evan Thomas, was granted a building lease by M.E. Boulton for the erection of not fewer than 20 or more than 27 houses in the area immediately adjacent to Soho House, the designs to be approved by M.E. Boulton's agent. These houses were to be built between September 1901 and September 1903, and probably involved the demolition of the remainder of the 18th-century service wing. M.E. Boulton had even less sentimental attachment to the house than his father had had, and was prepared to let housing encroach on the house to a much more significant extent. Evan and John Owen Thomas underleased Soho House and 4,129 square yards of land to Evan's wife Margaret in 1905. A school still occupied the house, known as Birmingham Central High School for Girls. A photograph of Soho House, probably taken on 17 August, the centenary of Matthew Boulton's death, indicates that the grounds had a much less neat appearance than in 1889, and the bedding scheme had been replaced by a rather rough croquet lawn. In 1911 the lease was transferred to Louisa Thomas, repairs were undertaken and a boarding house was opened. The house was featured in a *Country Life* article of 1915 as 'A Lesser Country House of the XVIIIth Century'.[33] This includes some interior photographs and a plan of the ground floor. Soho House continued as a boarding house, run by Louisa Thomas, after M.E. Boulton's death in 1914, after which the estate was administered on behalf of his two unmarried sisters by the Public Trustee.

Louisa Thomas died in 1923 and the boarding house business passed to her son, Clifford Thomas, who seems to have upgraded it, for from 1921 the house appears in *Kelly's Directory* as the *Soho Hall Hotel*. In 1927 the main rooms were photographed by Lewis and Randall (possibly as part of a campaign to persuade the city fathers to buy the house and open it as a museum).

Albert Tuck bought the lease from Clifford Thomas on 15 July 1929 and continued to run the hotel. It was Tuck's second hotel and was usually run by a manageress. Nos 5 and 7 Vicarage Road became extensions or annexes to the hotel in the 1930s.

47 *Photograph of Soho House, c.1909.*

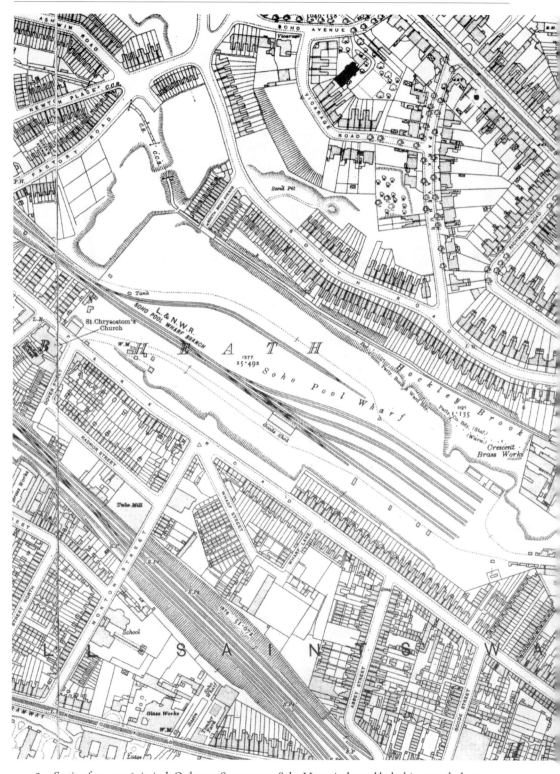

48   *Section from 1918 six-inch Ordnance Survey map. Soho House is shown blacked-in towards the top.*

During the 1930s an extension was added on the west side to provide bathroom facilities for the hotel. A photograph of the grounds of the hotel probably taken in 1955 indicates that the Hollins' lamp pedestals were still in situ then.

In 1955 the lease was transferred to the General Electric Company who used the building as a hostel for their apprentices, with part of the second floor used as a warden's flat. The wardens during this period, Mr and Mrs Harley, took an enthusiastic interest in the history of the house, and during their occupation excavated the 18th-century heating stove in the cellar and had the porch (accidentally demolished by a lorry during a Second World War blackout) rebuilt, using photographs to match it to the original. They also found fragments of the original drawing room fireplace in the garden, identified from a 1790s drawing of 'Chimney Piece in Mr Boulton's Drawing Room'.[34]

49 *Photograph of the driveway at Soho House, c.1955.*

The G.E.C. hostel was closed in 1961 and the City of Birmingham took over the lease. In 1963 the freehold of Soho House and the surrounding plot, including houses, was sold to the city by the trustees of M.E. Boulton. The building was subsequently acquired by the Police and became a hostel for single policemen in 1964, a new two-storey building being built alongside the house to provide additional accommodation. The police hostel closed on 16 February 1990 and the house and hostel block, along with the remaining 0.86 acres (0.348 hectares) of land, returned to city ownership as part of the City of Birmingham Heritage Development Plan, to ensure continued preservation of the house and to allow for future opening to the public.

The changes of occupancy and use documented in brief above mainly concern the house itself, but by the time Soho House became a school in 1893 there had also been significant changes to the gardens and park as building leases were granted.

Thus by 1900, the Soho Manufactory, the Mint, the service wing of Soho House, and the majority of Matthew Boulton's gardens and park had all disappeared – only the old house itself remained, now in a very different setting. A *Birmingham Mail*

article on Matthew Boulton's estate at Soho in 1903 observed that, 'in the very near future the whole of the historic Boulton estate at Handsworth will have been developed for building and other purposes.'[35] When a further lease for a pair of semi-detached villas was granted on the site of the carriage drive entrance in 1913 this eliminated the last of Matthew Boulton's planting. By this date the Soho House garden had been considerably reduced in size, though one feature of the house's former importance lingered on until the 1950s, the entrance driveway from Soho Avenue continuing to run to the front of the house, until this too was eliminated by extensions.

As all of this demonstrates, M.P.W. Boulton's policy of high-class development had certainly not continued into the 20th century and the reason for the move towards higher density housing lay in the consequences of the loss of the great pool and its development as coal yards. The sloping land of the old kitchen garden, the farmyard, the Mint and the winding walkways, was not developed until just before the First World War; its aspect over the coal depot, whose surroundings were described as 'as dingy as could be found anywhere in the city',[36] was not conducive to the building of large detached villas, and this area was finally developed with long streets of small terraced housing. Similar developments characterised the site of Shell Pool grounds, the pool having been drained in 1898. Remarkably, a part of the wooded grounds survived until the 1960s, having been added to the appropriately named detached villa, Woodleigh, in Park Avenue.

The large villas in their turn were subject to redevelopment in the second half of the 20th century, their gardens offering sites for flats, or they were converted to factories. By 1962 much of the area at the bottom of the estate, developed from 1849, had vanished under the tarmacadam of road-widening schemes. The coal yards gave way to a petroleum depot, and subsequently to Hockley Brook Trading Estate, sawmills and a scrap yard. The site of the Manufactory, not built on until the 20th century, was eventually developed as a lock factory, finally eradicating the workmen's gardens, once by the Manufactory, some of which were still evident in 1918. Likewise the guinea gardens on the Slade, laid out by M.R. Boulton,

50   *Photograph of the Slade Guinea Gardens, c.1890 just prior to redevelopment for building.*

were gradually diminished in size as successive development swallowed them up including the Soho, Handsworth and Perry Barr Railway which had truncated them by 1890 together with a branch line leading from the LNWR coal depot on Soho wharf on the site of the Pool. However, around 1890, just prior to being redeveloped, the Slade gardens were photographed and show the central access path, by this date called Slade Lane, together with the hedged enclosures for each garden. This photograph provides an extremely rare image of the detached gardens that were once so prevalent in Birmingham, and which Matthew Boulton and his son had provided for their workmen.

In 1794 when he was weighing up the pros and cons of buying the freehold of his estate, Matthew Boulton, in what was almost a prescient eulogy to a vanished garden, wrote that if he did not,

> the Consequences will be, That Houses, Workshops & other Nuisances may be built upon the Lawn facing the Parlour Windows ... I shall have the Mortification to see the Plantations & Shruberies which I have raised, Cut down & applied to other mens uses; and the Soil I have collected spread on other mens Grounds, I shall, with pain, see the Flower Garden I have formed, & its Temple, destroyed, my pools drained; my Cascade & Waterfalls no more please the Eye or the Ear ... The Monument I have raised to myself, with so much pains & Expence, I shall see Gliding upon the Wings of Time into the possession of other Families.[37]

POSTSCRIPT

Phillada Ballard and Val Loggie

After Soho House was acquired by Birmingham City Council in 1990 some urgent repairs were undertaken to the roof, and then planning began for its restoration and opening as a museum (*see* Plate 14). An adjacent building added by the Police was to be converted to a visitor centre and introductory gallery, while the house was to contain additional museum displays on the Boulton family and the Soho Manufactory. Period rooms were to reproduce Boulton's own decorative and furnishing schemes as closely as possible. Research in the Archives of Soho provided information on a wide range of topics which assisted with planning all these rooms. The house itself was also persuaded to give up its secrets, with archaeologists and specialists examining it in minute detail to determine changes in layout, and finding fragments of original wallpapers and paint finishes. These clues were all pulled together to create interiors as close as possible to those which would have been found in the house around 1800, after Boulton had undertaken his grand scheme and it was close to how he wanted it.

The refurbishment of a period house as a museum can be considered as incomplete if the setting is not treated as equally worthy of careful consideration. At Soho, although the house had been reduced in size the main portion remained, in marked contrast to the once extensive grounds, which had been reduced by successive building development to less than an acre. Soho House was, when the Museum acquired it in 1990, in effect an urban house set in a plot that would have been considered a 'town garden' in the late 18th century. At that time the owners of such properties did not regard size as an overwhelming constraint and included in their gardens many of the features found on larger estates. Carriage drives and paths were of gravel and irregular-shaped beds were planted with shrubs and herbaceous plants and set in lawns. Specimen trees were used and climbers were planted against the house. Garden buildings, statuary and seats were additional features.

Just as it had done for the house, research in the Soho Archives produced a mass of evidence for Matthew Boulton's garden and its progression over time.

Much information was obtained from the surviving nurserymen's bills, and from contemporary nurserymen's catalogues, of the plants he had used. Less apparent was how the plants were combined, as no planting plans had survived, if indeed there had ever been any. The surviving instructions for the Temple of Flora beds emphasised what was shown in the Phillp pictures and the contemporary gardening literature, that beds were planted in a tiered effect, with the tallest plants at the back descending to the lowest at the front. In many cases colour was provided by perennials, annuals and bulbs concentrated at the front of the border to provide a 'ribbon of colour'.

The decision was taken to lay out what remained of the garden in the style of the late 18th century, and to use only plants in cultivation at that time. This was not without difficulties, as 'period plants' are more difficult to obtain than the longer flowering and much more readily available modern cultivars. The planting method, which allowed for areas of bare soil between single plants or small groups of plants, caused puzzlement when compared to the modern practice of using blocks of colour and dense planting to suppress weeds. Such a garden takes time to establish and requires more precise and knowledgeable maintenance.

In Matthew Boulton's re-incarnated garden the plants have gained by not being constantly covered in soot from the coal fires formerly used for heating and cooking, let alone from the Mint and Manufactory. On the other hand, they have suffered to an extent from the attentions of the local domestic cat population.

The garden is not just a setting for the house, but a resource for learning about plants, their places of origin and dates of introduction, their characteristics as represented in their Latin names, and their uses.

The Hermitage, one of Matthew Boulton's garden buildings, was reconstructed based on John Phillp's drawings to represent the variety of features that Boulton had had at Soho and which had been lost over time (see Plate 15). There is one notable exception to these losses: the Museum has been able to acquire the pair of Sphinxes that gave their name to the walk made in 1796 leading to the kitchen garden. These are currently on display at Birmingham Museums & Art Gallery but in the longer term it is planned to return them to Soho.

Soho House opened as a museum in 1995 and continues to welcome visitors to Handsworth, as Matthew Boulton did 200 years ago.

ENDNOTES

ABBREVIATIONS

BAH – Birmingham Archives & Heritage Services at Birmingham Central Library, where the following collections are held:
  MS 3782 – Matthew Boulton Papers (MBP).
  MS 3219 – James Watt Papers (JWP).
  MS 3147 – Boulton & Watt Papers (B&W).

BMAG – Birmingham Museums & Art Gallery.
M.B. – Matthew Boulton.
M.R.B. – Matthew Robinson Boulton.

INTRODUCTION

1. It was probably Mary Boulton (1731-68) who lived at Soho House with her mother in 1762-3, because Boulton's other sister, Catherine (b.1735), was married to Thomas Mynd by then (their first child, Nancy Mynd, was born in 1763).
2. For further information on visitors to Soho and industrial espionage, see Peter Jones, *Industrial Enlightenment: Science, technology and culture in Birmingham and the West Midlands* (Manchester, 2009), and (same author) 'I had Lords and Ladys to wait on yesterday …' in Mason, S. (ed.), *Matthew Boulton: Selling what all the World Desires* (Yale, 2009).
3. James Boswell, *Life of Dr Johnson* (1791).
4. MS 3782/12/108/70, notebook 1795.
5. Jacques *Georgian Gardens*, p.106; J.D. Hunt and P. Willis (eds), *The Genius of the Place* (1975), p.245.
6. MS 3782/British Coinage Official Correspondence Vol. I, Thomas Lack – M.B., 5 February 1801.
7. Collection of drawings and watercolours known as the Phillp Album, Birmingham Museums & Art Gallery, BMAG 2003.0031. *See* Chapter Three for further information on Phillp's life and work.
8. MS 3782/12/46/196, Fanny de Luc – M.B., June 1801.
9. MS 3782/12/38/129, William Herschel – M.B., July 1793.

CHAPTER ONE

1. James Bisset, *Poetic Survey Round Bimingham*, published with his *Magnificent Directory of Birmingham* (1800); a second edition, entitled *Bisset's Magnificent Guide or Grand Copperplate Directory For the Town of Birmingham* was published in 1808.
2. BAH 608098/A, Botham's Plan of Handsworth Heath, 1794.
3. MS 3782/6/6/188, receipt from Rev. John Birch, 28 August 1769.
4. MS 3782/6/3, House Cash Book, 1768-80.
5. Kenneth Morgan (ed.), *An American Quaker in the British Isles: The Travel Journals of Jabez Maud Fisher1775-1779* (Oxford, 1992), p.253.
6. MS 3782/12/111/150, 'Considerations upon the Propriety of buying Soho … First, as it relates to my Health & Happiness;

and secondly, as it relates to my Interest'. In Matthew Boulton's hand, n.d. [1794].
7. MS 3782/12/60/265, Memorandum, dispute between B. and F., n.d. [1766].
8. Ibid.
9. MS 3782/12/108/70, Notebook, 1795.
10. Birmingham Museums & Art Gallery, Verse in Phillp Album . BMAG 2003.31.81 (*see also* Chapter Three, p.54-5).
11. MS 3782/12/107/6, Matthew Boulton's diary, 1771.
12. David Jacques, *Georgian Gardens, The Reign of Nature* (1983), p.104.
13. MS 3782/12/108/7, Notebook 8 (1772).
14. Jacques *Georgian Gardens*, p.106; J.D. Hunt and P. Willis (eds), *The Genius of the Place* (1975), p.308.
15. Christie's, *Catalogue of Books from the Library of Matthew Boulton and his Family*, 12 December 1986, lot 94.
16. Copy with Matthew Boulton's book plate in a private collection.
17. Norman and Beryl Kitz, *Pains Hill Park* (Cobham, 1984).
18. MS 3782/12/108/7, Notebook 8, 1772.
19. Schofield, R., *The Lunar Society of Birmingham: A Social History of Provincial Science and Industry in Eighteenth-Century England* (Oxford, 1966), p.24.
20. MS 3782/13/36/81, letter, M.B. – M.R.B., 27 August 1792. Boulton writes to his son 'I approve of [your sister] going to the Leasowes.' This must have been quite a short visit, for he also knew that she was going on to visit their friends the Turners, at Shenstone near Lichfield, from where she wrote to him about attending Lichfield Races and services at Lichfield Cathedral. (MS 3782/13/38/7, Miss Boulton – M.B., 9 September 1792).
21. Dianne Barre, 'Sir Samuel Hellier and his garden buildings: part of the Midlands "garden circuit" in the 1760s-70s?', *Garden History*, vol. 32, no. 2, 2008, 310-27.
22. MS 3782/6/3, House Cash Book, 1768-80.
23. MS 3782/14/76/33, M.B. – Miss Anne Boulton, 25 December 1796.
24. Adam Murray, *General View of the Agriculture of the County of Warwick* (1818), p.320.

25. MS 3782/12/44/22, Rev. Thomas Lane – M.B., 17 January 1799.
26. MS 3782/12/59/210, William Cheshire – M.B., 18 April 1801.
27. MS 3782/6/3, House Cash Book, 1768-80.
28. *See* Note 16.
29. MS 3782/12/23/138, William Envill – M.B., 12 August 1769.
30. MS 3782/6/185, M.R.B. Land and House Agents Ledger, 1833-42.
31. MS 3782/6/3, House Cash Book, 1768-80.
32. MS 3782/6/3, House Cash Book, 1768-80.
33. Anon. 1802, xxi, in *The Concise History of Birmingham* (1815).
34. Andrew Oliver (ed.), *The Journal of Samuel Curwen, Loyalist* (Cambridge, Mass., 1972), p.348.
35. MS 3782/6/3, House Cash Book, 1768-80.
36. MS 3782/6/17, Household Ledger no. 3, 1800-7, Garden and Plantation account.
37. MS 3782/6/3, House Cash Book, 1768-80.
38. Birmingham Archives & Heritage MS1682/8/10, Architectural Drawings from Great Tew, formerly Lot 38, item 3, in Christie's *Catalogue of Fine Architectural Drawings and Watercolours*, 16 December 1986.
39. MS 3782/12/108/70, Notebook, 1795.
40. MS 3782/6/92, Charles Glover's Accounts, 1795.
41. MS 3782/6/3, House Cash Book, 1768-80.
42. *See* Note 40.
43. MS 3782/12/57/25, M.B. – M.R.B., 25 September 1788.
44. MS 3782/6/3, House Cash Book, 1768-80.
45. MS 3782/12/61/50, Samuel Garbett – Mrs Barker, 13 July 1783; MS 3782/4/123/Letterbook 1, James Watt – Joseph Fry, 22 July 1783.
46. Private Collection, Patty Fothergill's diary entry for 8 August 1793, quoted in Mason, S., *The Hardware Man's Daughter* (2005), pp.95-6.
47. MS 3782/12/108/5, Notebook 6 (1768) and MS 3782/12/108/7, Notebook 8 (1772).
48. MS 3782/6/3, House Cash Book, 1768-80.
49. MS 3782/1/27/20, Alexander Aubert – Boulton and Fothergill, 25 September 1778.
50. Muirhead, J.P., *The Life of James Watt, with Selections from his Correspondence* (London, 1858), pp. 250-1.
51. *See* Note 50.
52. Christie's *Catalogue of Books from the Library of Matthew Boulton and his Family*, 12 December 1986, lot 116.
53. MS 3782/6/92, Charles Glover's accounts, 1793.
54. MS 3782/6/3, House Cash Book, 1768-80.
55. MS 3782/6/3, House Cash Book, 1768-80.
56. MS 3782/12/81/50, 51, Josiah Wedgwood – M.B., 29 April and 1 May 1785.
57. MS 3782/12/107/4, Diary, 1769.
58. MS 3147/5/714a.
59. MS 3147/5/1469.
60. MS 3782/6/96, p.93.
61. MS 3782/6/96, Benjamin Wyatt's accounts, 1797-8.
62. MS 3782/12/57/25, M.B. – M.R.B., 25 September 1788.
63. MS 3782/13/39/126, M.B. – James Watt, 15 May 1804.
64. MS 3782/6/7/118, bill from George Withers, 5 April 1788, 'Trenching ground and banking for clumps of trees on Handsworth Common', five men for six days, three men for six and a half days, one man for five days and one for three and a half days, total £4 17s. 7d.
65. MS 3782/6/193/31, bill from John Green, 1787.
66. MS 3782/6/3, House Cash Book, 1768-80.
67. MS 3782/6/6/7, J. Bramall – M.B., 14 February 1768.
68. MS 3782/6/193/43(d), bill from Brunton and Forbes, 1 January 1788.
69. MS 3782/6/193/43(b), bill from Brunton and Forbes, 18 April 1788.
70. MS 3782/14/76/3, M.B. – Miss Anne Boulton, 23 June 1784.
71. Private collection. Illustrated in Mason, S., *The Hardware Man's Daughter: Matthew Boulton and his 'Dear Girl'* (Chichester, 2005), plate 17.
72. MS 3782/6/193/43, Letter, James Hunter – M.B., 19 April 1788, with accompanying bill from Brunton & Forbes dated 18 April 1788.
73. MS3782/6/192/100, bill from Brunton and Forbes, 9 April 1783.
74. MS 3782/6/190/201, bill from James Gordon – M.B., 6 November 1766.
75. MS 3782/2/13, Inventory, 22 June 1782.
76. MS 3782/6/3, House Cash Book, 1768-80.
77. MS 3782/12/108/70, Notebook, 1795.
78. Ibid.
79. MS 3782/6/3, House Cash Book, 1768-80. In 1776 the gardener's bill included 13s. 9d. for 165 yards of dwarf box.
80. MS 3782/12/59/163, William Cheshire – M.B., Soho, 23 May 1797.
81. MS 3782/6/6/741, bill, Minire and Mason – Matthew Boulton, £2 4s. 1d., 7 February 1772.
82. MS 3782/12/108/92, Notebook, 1801.
83. MS 3782/6/3, House Cash Book, 1768-80.
84. MS 3782/6/109-26, House miscellaneous loose bills [MBP264], William Farnol bill, 1771-2.
85. MS 3782/6/3, House Cash Book, 1768-80, bill for 8s. to Mr Pavel for carriage of M.B.'s hothouse, 9 July 1773.
86. MS 3782/12/108/12, Notebook, 1776-7.
87. MS 3782/6/7/101, bill from Benjamin Cox – M.B., 23 March 1788.
88. MS 3782/6/3, House Cash Book, 1768-80.
89. Stratford RO Map ER23/131/1, 2 or 16.
90. MS3782/6/3, House Cash Book, 1768-80.
91. MS3782/6/3, House Cash Book, 1768-80.
92. MS 3782/6/200/1, List of payments made for time worked by William Carless, John White and others, on the menagerie and grounds at Soho House, 1776.
93. MS 3782/6/3, House Cash Book, 1768-80.
94. MS 3782/6/6/53, bill, William Bromley (gardener) – [Matthew Boulton], 24 December 1768.
95. MS 3783/6/8, House Cash Book, 1768-80.
96. MS 3782/6/3, House Cash Book, 1768-80.
97. MS 3782/6/4, House Cash Book, 1781-91.

CHAPTER TWO

1. MS 3782/12/111/150, 'Considerations upon the Propriety of buying Soho … First, as it relates to my Health & Happiness; and secondly, as it relates to my Interest'. In Matthew Boulton's hand, n.d. [1794].
2. MS 3782/12/108/70, Notebook, 1795.
3. MS 3782/12/68/98, Copy letter M.B. – Charlotte Matthews, 23 Nov 1795.
4. MS 3782/12/111/145, Statement of Soho Dr and Credt Soho Premises Land and Buildings value from suppose abt. 1796.
5. MS 3782/13/149/181, George Birch – M.B., draft notice to quit, 10 December 1794.
6. MS 3782/12/37/54, William Withering – M.B., 14 March 1792.
7. MS 3792/12/39/92, M.B. – Heneage Legge, 7 April 1794.
8. MS 3782/12/39/250, H. Whateley – M.B., 13 September 1794.
9. MS 3147/11/3/17/5, M.B. – James Watt, 3 May 1794.
10. *See* Note 1.
11. MS 3782/12/108/70, 75, and 92, Notebooks for 1795-1801.
12. MS 3782/12/108/68, Notebook, 1793-99.
13. MS 3782/12/108/70, Notebook 70, 1795.
14. As above.
15. BAH MS275a/489, Robins Collection.
16. MS 3782/6/195/15, W. Hollins account 1795-6; BAH MS1682/8/11, Christie 1986b.

17. MS 3219/7/1/28, Anne Watt – Gregory Watt, 13 November 1796.
18. MS 3782/6/18, Ledger 5.
19. MS 3782/12/108/75, Notebook, 1797.
20. MS 3782/12/108/92, Notebook, 1801-3.
21. *See* Note 18.
22. MS 3782/12/108/70, Notebook, 1795.
23. BAH MS1682/2/1; 1682/6; Christie 1986b.
24. BAH MS1682/8/7; Christie 1986b.
25. MS 3782/12/49/154, William Withering junior – M.B., 11 May 1804.
26. MS 3782/13/36/54, M.B. – M.R.B., 16 May 1791; MS 3782/6//92, Charles Glover's account, 1794-5; MS 3782/6/98, B. Wyatt's account, 1800-1.
27. MS 3782/6/13/22, Journal, 1805-8.
28. MS 3782/6/99, unnamed account, January – October 1801. The boathouse cost £36 2s. 7d. [MBP 446].
29. MS 3782/6/195/6, W. Hollins account, 1795-6.
30. MS 3782/6/195/6, bill from E.G. Saunders, August 1795.
31. Cooke, Ivor Guest Hamel, *William Garland: The Nineteenth-Century Diaries of a Birmingham Engineer* (London, 1997).
32. MS 3219/7/1/26, Annie Watt – Gregory Watt, 10 November 1795.
33. MS 3782/6/97, B. Wyatt account, 1797-1801.
34. MS 3782/12/108/70, Notebook, 1795.
35. MS 3782/6/3 and MS 3782/6/4, House Cash books, 1768-80 and 1781-91.
36. MS 3782/6/96, p.94; MS1682/8/1.
37. MS 3782/12/108/75, Notebook, 1797-1801.
38. MS 3782/12/108/68, Notebook, 1793-1803.
39. MS 3782/12/47/78, Cornelius Dixon – William Cheshire, 6 March 1802.
40. MS 3782/6/97, B. Wyatt, Soho House Building account, 1798-1801.
41. MS 3782/12/108/70, Notebook, 1795.
42. MS 3782/12/108/75, Notebook, 1797.
43. MS 3782/12/108/75, Notebook, 1795.
44. MS 3782/14/76/44, M.B. – Anne Boulton, 24 April 1801.
45. MS 3782/12/59/221, William Cheshire – M.B., 9 June 1801.
46. MS 3782/14/76/49, M.B. – Anne Boulton, 19 June 1801.
47. MS 3782/12/108/92, Notebook, 1801-3.
48. MS 3782/12/108/70, Notebook, 1795.
49. MS 3782/12/108/92, Notebook, 1801-3.
50. Boulton bought Thornhill House for his son's use in 1799, but Matt did not choose to live there. In 1803 Boulton was considering letting it to James Watt junior, but when his daughter and her doctor, Dr John Carmichael, announced their intention to marry he gave the house to her. The engagement did not last for long and once again Thornhill House was let. From 1808 the tenant was James Watt junior. He continued to live there until 1818, when he moved to Aston Hall to make way for Miss Boulton to take up residence at Thornhill when she left Soho House following her brother's marriage.
51. MS 3782/6/92, Chas Glover accounts, 1798, Wm Lowe roses and shrubs.
52. MS 3782/6/92, Chas Glover accounts, 1799, J. Blaksley roses.
53. MS 3782/12/108/75, Notebook, 1797-1801.
54. MS 3782/12/108/92, Notebook, 1801-3.
55. MS 3782/12/85/131a, M.B. – James Wyatt, 6 July 1796.
56. MS 3782/6/15, Household Ledger, 1796-97.
57. MS 3782/12/59/208, William Cheshire – M.B., 18 August 1800.
58. MS 3782/12/108/92, Notebook, 1801-3.
59. MS 3782/14/76/45, M.B. –Miss Anne Boulton, 1 May 1801; MS 3782/14/76/48, M.B. – Miss Anne Boulton, 7 June 1801.
60. MS 3782/20/4, Ram for Mr Boulton's garden, June 1798.
61. MS 3782/12/59/227, William Cheshire – M.B., 4 July 1803.
62. MS 3782/12/108/92, Notebook, 1801-3.
63. MS 3782/13/41/140, William Cheshire – M.R.B., 14 February 1809.

64. MS 3782/12/59/213, William Cheshire – M.B., 29 April 1801.
65. MS 3782/12/59/210, William Cheshire – M.B., 18 April 1801.
66. MS 3782/12/59/210, 211, 212, 216, 217, William Cheshire – M.B., 18 April, 25 April, 28 April, 13 May, 21 May 1801.
67. MS 3782/6/106, 1798-1811/26a, payment of Tithe to Rev. T. Lane, 13 July 1796.
68. MS 3782/14/76/35, M.B. – Miss Anne Boulton, 11 September 1800.
69. MS 3782/12/59/220, William Cheshire – M.B., 1 June 1801.
70. MS 3782/12/108/92, Notebook 1801.
71. MS 3782/13/149/25, Memorandum. Produce of 1805 and estimated value thereof, 1806.
72. MS 3782/6/136/7, William Chesire – M.B., 22 Jul 1807.
73. MS 3782/13/149/67, Estimate of labour costs required to maintain the gardens, n.d.
74. MS 3782/12/108/68, Notebook, 'Agriculture', 1793-99.
75. MS 3782/12/59/163, William Cheshire – M.B., Soho, 23 May 1797.
76. MS 3782/12/50/171, draft letter, M.B. – James Crummer, September 1805.
77. MS 3782/6/136/80, copy letter in William Cheshire's hand, M.B. – Mr Robinson, 29 May 1807.
78. BAH, G.H. Osborne's newspaper cuttings relating to Boulton, Watt and Murdoch, *Aris's Brmingham Gazette*, 5 April 1802.
79. The Rev. Warton, 1802, quoted in A. and P. Burton, *The Green Bag Travellers: Britain's First Tourists* (1978), p.95.
80. BAH397963, M.B. Centenary, 17 August 1909, newscuttings, 1788-1911.

Chapter Three

1. The research for this work was carried out as part of an AHRC-funded PhD co-supervised by the University of Birmingham and Birmingham Museums & Art Gallery.
2. MS 3782/12/45/450, John Phillp – M.B., n.d., 1800, states that he will be 22 at midsummer. However, burial record 14 July 1815 for John Phillp states he was thirty-three. BRL St Paul's Birmingham Burials, 1813-8, DRO 35/29, page 83 no. 658. I am grateful to Nicholas Molyneux for the record of Phillp's death.
3. MS 3782/12/38/10, George C. Fox – M.B., 25 January 1793.
4. MS 3782/12/38/20, M.B. – George C. Fox, 16 February 1793.
5. MS 3782/12/38/37, George C. Fox – M.B., 2 March 1793.
6. MS 3782/12/38/160, George C. Fox– M.B., 23 Sept 1793.
7. H.W. Dickinson, *Matthew Boulton* (Cambridge, 1937), p.99.
8. Boulton's biographer Dickinson accepted that Phillp was Boulton's son but gave no evidence: 'he was reputed, and we believe rightly, to be Boulton's natural son.' (Dickinson, H.W., *Matthew Boulton* (Cambridge University Press, 1937), p.147.) Mason outlines the evidence and states that it is not conclusive (Mason, S., *The Hardware Man's Daughter: Matthew Boulton and his 'Dear Girl'* (Chichester, 2005), p.223 n.28.) Doty takes the entirely practical line that this was a persistent rumour but that the correspondence between Boulton and Fox makes the link unlikely: 'Unless Fox had been deliberately misled (or unless he and Boulton had agreed on an elaborate written deception for the benefit of future historians), I cannot see how any blood connection between Matthew Boulton and John Phillp can be assumed.' (Doty, Richard, *The Soho Mint & the Industrialization of Money* (Smithsonian Institution, 1998), p.49.) Brian Gould, who spent a year working on the Matthew Boulton Papers (now known as MS3782), found nothing to 'substantiate the rumour.'
9. Brian Gould, 'John Phillp: Birmingham Artist (1778-1815), unpublished typescript. Copy in files at Soho House Museum.
10. MS 3782/12/2/23, M.B. – James Adam, 1 October 1770; 'Memoirs of M. Boulton Esq F.R.S.', *Caledonian Mercury*, 4 September 1809; Dickinson, p.60.
11. MS 3782/12/98, Papers relating to Paris journey, 1786.
12. MS3782/12/60/3,5,6,9, John Fothergill – M.B., 1762, regarding

Mr [Benjamin] Green engraving chapes; 3782/12/108/14, M.B., Notebook, 1779, Holland, p.26 regarding leaving books of plated goods.

13. Martin Ellis, 'Francis Eginton' in *Oxford DNB online*, accessed 24 June 2007; Anthony Griffiths, 'Notes on Early Aquatint in England and France' in *Print Quarterly*, IV, 1987, 3, pp.256-70; Val Loggie, 'Picturing Soho', in Mason (ed.), *Matthew Boulton: Selling What All the World Desires* (Yale UP, 2009).

14. Kenneth Quickenden, 'Boulton and Fothergill's Silversmiths', *The Silver Society Journal*, No. 7, Autumn 1995. I am grateful to him for discussion on this subject.

15. Dickinson, H.W., *Matthew Boulton* (1936), pp.146-7.

16. MS3782/6/195/7, William Hollins bill, 30 June 1795, endorsed 'Hollins the Stone cutter'.

17. Michael Fisher, 'William Hollins' in *Oxford DNB online*, accessed 24 June 2007; *Aris's Gazette*, 10 August 1801. I am grateful to Victoria Osborne for this reference.

18. BMAG 2003.0031.77; BMAG 2003.0031.71.

19. MS 3219/7/1/4, Jessy and Ann Watt to Gregory Watt, 1 March 1793. MS 3782/7/10/549, Joseph Barber's bill, 1792; MS 3782/12/107/24, M.B. Diary, 1796.

20. Kim Sloan, Alexander and John Robert Cozens, *The Poetry of Landscape* (Yale UP, 1986), p.29; BMAG 2003.0031.91.

21. 3782/12/41/203, Robert Andrew Riddell – M.B., 15 June 1796. I am grateful to Peter Jones for drawing my attention to this letter.

22. City of Hereford Archaeology Unit, Soho House, November 1990, pp.41-3.

23. 3782/12/108/70, M.B. Notebook, 1795.

24. The location of Phillp's journal for this visit is no longer known but typescript notes on it by Brian Gould are in the files at Soho House.

25. Frances Collard, 'Thomas Hope's Furniture' in Watkin and Hewat-Jaboor (eds), *Thomas Hope: Regency Designer* (Yale UP, 2008), p.61.

26. MS3782/13/44/113, press copy, M.B. – John Woodward, 25 January 1805.

27. MS3782/12/59/230, Richard Chippendall – M.B., 1 January 1807.

28. MS3782/13/41/54, Richard Chippendall – John Hodges, 15 June 1808.

29. The two items dated 1792, both seascapes, predate Phillp's arrival at Soho in spring 1793 aged about fourteen, *see above*. The fact that both of these images are seascapes is presumably influenced by his residence in Falmouth. One item is dated 1793, a mountainous landscape with a lake in the foreground and is a copy of a plate in William Gilpin's *Observations on the River Wye*. It is not clear where Phillp was when he did this painting but it seems more likely that he would have had access to a copy of Gilpin's book at Soho although the known Boulton copy of Wye was the fifth edition of 1800, *see* Chapter Two.

30. This work formed part of and was made possible by the NOF-funded Digital Handsworth Project and allowed the material to be made available online.

31. Phillada Ballard, *Soho House Gardens 1761-1809; Report for the Heritage Development Department Birmingham Museums & Art Gallery* (1992), identified a number of the views of the estate, particularly the garden buildings.

32. Ballard, 1992; George Demidowicz, *The Soho Industrial Buildings: Manufactory Mint and Foundry* (forthcoming). These works have also been used extensively for the present author's forthcoming PhD at the University of Birmingham.

33. BAH LF54.81 373482, *Collectanea Delineatum a Johanne Phillp*, 1792-1811.

34. Other images which use this view include a plate in Swinney's *Birmingham Directory* of 1773 and an aquatint of the same year by Francis Eginton, British Museum 1978,1216.3.1. A reworked version of this aquatint is one of the items in the Phillp album so Phillp was certainly aware of it and it is possible that it was Phillp who reworked Eginton's original plate. For further discussion on such views and how they were used see Val Loggie,

'Picturing Soho' in Shena Mason (ed.), *Matthew Boulton: Selling What all the World Desires* (Yale UP, 2009), pp. 22-30.

35. Aerial perspective is the creation of the illusion of distance in a landscape painting by making objects paler and bluer the further they are from the viewer. Repoussoir is the placing of an object in the right or left foreground so it acts as a framing element, leading the viewer's eye back into the composition. 'The Concise Oxford Dictionary of Art Terms' in *Oxford Art Online*, accessed 15 March 2009.

36. T. Radclyffe's engraving after F. Calvert in William West, *Picturesque Views, and Descriptions of Cities, Towns, Castles, Mansions … in Staffordshire and Shropshire*, 1830, shows Soho from the Nineveh Road and makes clear the wooded setting which would have grown further by this date.

37. 3782/6/133/30, Copy letter, William Cheshire – Dr Solomon, 23 January 1804.

38. It is also unclear whether the portrait bust at the centre of the decoration was intended to be of Boulton himself, or whether it was just a generic figure.

39. Phillp Album, BMAG 2003.0031.81.

40. Boulton did not settle at Soho in 1775, but 1766. As some work had been undertaken in 1772 and the garden would not have been the barren heath the poet describes it is likely that 1772 is a mistake either by the poet or by Phillp in his transcription.

41. 3782/12/34/171, Humphry Repton – M.B., 21 Sept 1789.

42. BMAG 2003.31.27, The paper has been trimmed but the tops of 'M', 'tt' and 'B' are visible.

CHAPTER FOUR

1. Private collections. These include a watercolour view of Shell Pool by Hugh Boulton and a pencil sketch of the same pool by Katherine Boulton.

2. Letter, K.E.M. – B.M., 27/7/1880 or 81, private collection.

3. MS 3782/13/14/84, James Royds (Rochdale) – M.R.B., 18 August 1810, reference for Alexander Stephenson; MS 3782/6/ general correspondence, 1810/175, W. Cheshire – S. Partridge, 14 December 1810.

4. MS 3782/6/139/37, Alexander Stevenson – Biggs, 6 October 1810.

5. MS 3782/6/139/39, M.R. Boulton – William Butler, 10 October 1810; MS 3782/6/139/204, M.R. Boulton – Mr Taylor, 10 October 1810.

6. Though it appears that Stephenson had already made his choice at Butler's nursery. MS 3782/6/139/40, William Butler – M.R. Boulton, 29 October 1810.

7. MS 3782/MRB/private correspondence, 1809/4, 5, 6, 7, 8, 9, 11, 12, 14-22, October 1810.

8. MS 3782/13/16/102, William Cheshire, Soho – Rev. H.G.D. Yate (Bromsberrow, co. Glos.), 1 November 1811 and ff. letters.

9. MS 3782/13/149/50, List. Fruit trees in orchard at Heathfield, from James Watt, 1812. Includes 48 named varieties of apples and 17 varieties of pears. On the second page is a further list of 24 named apple trees at Mr Smith's, Craighead, near Hamilton.

10. MS 3782/13/149/45, List, 7 November 1812. Docketed: List of Fruit-Trees & other Memoranda for the Gardiner (Mr Beahan) by which to make his selection at Mr Butlers, Prescot.

11. MS 3782/13/149/41 & 42, plans of orchard, February 1812.

12. MS 3147/5/1469, Plans of Mr Boulton's house; for list of trees *see* Note 10.

13. MS 3782/13/149/60, 'Pomona Sohoniensis', 1811-21. List of numerous fruit trees and notes on their cultivation, cropping, quality of fruit, etc.

14. MS 3782/13/149/64, memorandum, n.d.

15. MS 3782/13/149/65, memorandum, n.d.

16. MS 3782/13/149/43, List. February 1812. Eighty-nine fruit trees ordered in February 1811.

17. MS 3782/9/4, Robert Niven (Great Tew) – Zaccheus Walker (Soho Mint), 22 March 1819, docketed. 'Writes for cuttings of apple-trees.' (Reply to this: MS 3782/9/2, Great Tew letterbook,

1816-44, Z. Walker – Mr Niven, Soho, 24 March 1819).

18. MS 3782/13/149/46 & 48, George Mynd – Zaccheus Walker, November 1812.

19. Graham Stuart Thomas, *The Graham Stuart Thomas Rose Book* (1994), p.310.

20. MS 3782/13/149/51, bill, Lee Kennedy (Hammersmith) – M.R. Boulton, 25 October 1813.

21. MS 3782/13/149/54, 4 December 1813, listing plants to be obtained from Gordon, Forsyth & Co.

22. MS 3782/13/149/57, 1813. Docketed: 'Catalogue of Flower-seeds &c &c sown in the Garden & the Flower-borders at Soho by J. Beahan'. [283 varieties, some in multiple quantities.]

23. Cooke, I.G.H., *The Nineteenth Century Diaries of a Birmingham Engineer* (1997), p.12.

24. BAHS, G.H. Osborne's Newspaper cuttings on Boulton, Watt and Murdock, *Aris's Birmingham Gazette*, 13 June 1814.

25. MS 3782/6/106/7, bill from Lee and Kennedy, 28 March 1818.

26. MS 3782/6/106/7, bill from J. Moore, February-August 1820.

27. MS 3782/6/185, pp.24 and 86.

28. F.W. Hackwood, *Handsworth: Old and New* (Birmingham, 1908), p.2; BRL 172745, Report of the Trial of Boulton V. Crowther [1824].

29. Cooke, *Birmingham Engineer*, p.15.

30. Private collection, Katherine Elizabeth Boulton – 'Diddle' (Anne Robinson Boulton), Soho, 27 October 1830.

31. MS 3782/6/185, p.90; MS 3782/6/185, p.90.

32. Private Collection, Katherine Boulton's Diaries, 1841-3.

33. Private Collection, Katherine E. Boulton – M.P.W.B., Soho, 11 January 1843.

34. MS 3782/6/185, p.7.

35. MS 3782/6/185, p.23, 9 May 1836.

36. MS 3782/13/149/26.

37. MS 3782/6/185, pp.59 and 104.

38. MS 3782/6/185, p.54.

39. MS 3782/11, Chubb letters, gardener's note for 14 June 1845.

40. Tithe Apportionment Parish of St Thomas, St Martin and All Saints, Birmingham, parcel 244, 1849.

41. MS 3782/6/182/1-283, Soho Desmene lands and Homestead 1821. The Upper and Lower Slade are described as 'in hand' and the acreage is 7a 1r 7p; MS 3782/6/153, Staffs and Warwks Estates rent roll, 1825-38; In 1856 M.P.W. Boulton received an annual rental of £46 6s. 7d. for the 'old workmen's gardens' and £53 13s. for the Slade gardens – MS 3782/6/182, Rentals of Soho Estate. An agreement for renting one of the Slade gardens has survived, in 1851 Thomas Workman agreed an annual rent of £1 8s (MS 3782/6/182, Land and House Agents' memoranda, 1806-63).

42. MS 3782/200/9, M.R.B., 1815, copied from Snape's plan No. 1; also MS 3782/12/108/70, Notebook, 1795.

43. MS 3782/13/149/33, Notebook on timber auction at Soho Park, 8 January 1833.

44. BAHS, BRL 17969, Boulton Estate Act, 1874.

45. Cartwright-Hignett, Elizabeth, *Lili at Aynhoe* (London, 1989).

46. Oxfordshire Record Office, Indenture Li XX/VIII/14.

47. Letter, K.E.M. – B.M., 28/7/1880 or 81, private collection.

48. MS 3782/10/29, steward or other servant's Notebook, 1847-9. Although M.R. Boulton had built a new library at Tew in the 1830s, he had never moved the books there from Soho, but in 1848 they were at last taken there. On 5 July 1848 a large quantity of silver and plate was given into the care of C. Crotchley, the butler at Great Tew, by Edward Price, the steward at Soho (MS 3782/11/Chubb correspondence).

49. *Birmingham Journal*, 28 July and 4 August 1849.

50. Birmingham Archives & Heritage, 664418, Boulton, Watt & Murdock newscuttings, 11 September 1911.

CHAPTER FIVE

1. MS 3782/20/4/54.

2. BRL 17969, Boulton Estate Act.

3. MS 3782/20/4.

4. MS 3782/11/Chubb, copies, 1849, C.J. Chubb – M.P.W.B., 1 May 1849; MS 3782/11/Chubb letters, M.P.W.B. – C.J.C., 15 May 1850.

5. MS 3782/11/Chubb letters/M.P.W.B. – C.J. Chubb, 10 June 1850.

6. MS 3782/11/Chubb letters/E. Price – C.J. Chubb, 19 November 1850.

7. MS 3782/6/182, Land and House Agents' memoranda, 1805-63, memorandum concerning Toy's lease of the Soho Manufactory, 29 September 1852.

8. MS 3782/6/182, Land and House Agents' memoranda, 1805-63, memorandum concerning review of Toy's lease, 22 September 1853.

9. *The Engineer*, 2 July 1858, p.17.

10. BAH, 369956.

11. Boulton Estate Act, 1874.

12. MS 3782/20/4, Skidmore agreement to build houses on Soho Hill.

13. BAH maps, 134251, map of Birmingham and outlying parishes by Henry Blood, 1857.

14. J.P. Muirhead, *The Life of James Watt with Selections from his Correspondence* (London, 1858), p.253.

15. Handsworth Historical Society, *A History of Handsworth part 4*; Anon., *St Michael's Church Handsworth Centenary 1855-1955* (Handsworth or ?Birmingham, 1955), pp.5-9.

16. MS 3782/13/149/146, Inventory of old furniture at Soho House when Mr Toy came, N.d; MS 3782/13/149/117, Specification of painting and papering required, 11 June 1860; MS 3782/13/149/119, Estimate of repairs and alterations, 18 June 1860.

17. MS 3782/11/Chubb papers, Vouchers for Cash payments, 1850; MS 3782/11/Chubb papers Disbursements Soho house and Estate, 1850-3.

18. MS 3782/13/149/114, Memorandum, repairs etc. needed at Soho House, 1 June 1860.

19. MS 3782/13/149/133, Specification, n.d. Work to be done at Soho House.

20. Katharine Elizabeth Muirhead (née Boulton) – Beatrix Muirhead, 28 July 1880/1 (private collection).

21. BAH, BCC uncatalogued plans, letter from W. Morgan, 1853, attached to plan of Soho Park.

22. MS 3782/20/4.

23. MS 3782/6/182, Land and House Agents' memoranda, 1805-63.

24. BAH, L65.225 66 4418, *Birmingham Weekly Post*, 10 September 1927.

25. Dent, R.K., *Old and New Birmingham*, vol. 3, p.567. The Lifeboat was subsequently stationed on the Lincolnshire coast.

26. SRO D564, Thynne & Thynne Soho Estate Records.

27. BAH, Osborne Newscuttings, *Birmingham Evening News*, 5 August 1875.

28. Staffordshire Record Office, D564, Thynne & Thynne Soho Estate records.

29. BAH, L65.225 66 4418, *Birmingham Weekly Post*, 6 September 1919.

30. BAH, Osborne Newscuttings Handsworth, vol. 3, *Birmingham Gazette*, 4 April 1882.

31. *See* Note 28 above.

32. Section from 1885 OS map.

33. A.T. Bolton, 'A Lesser Country House of the XVIIIth Century, Matthew Boulton's Home, near Birmingham', *Country Life*, 6 November 1915.

34. MS 3147/5/1469.

35. BAH 286526, Osborne Newscuttings, B&W, 1903.

36. BAH, L65.225 66 4418, *Birmingham Weekly Post*, 6 September 1919.

37. MS 3782/12/111/150, 'Considerations upon the Propriety of buying Soho', 1794.

BIBLIOGRAPHY

Ballard, Phillada, 'Soho House Gardens', unpublished research report for Birmingham Museums & Art Gallery (1992)

Ballard, Phillada, 'A Historical Approach to the Re-modelling of the Gardens of Soho House, Birmingham' (unpublished report, 1993)

Ballard, Phillada, 'Planting for Soho House Gardens' (unpublished report, 1995)

Bolton, A.T., 'A Lesser Country House of the XVIIIth Century, Matthew Boulton's Home near Birmingham', in *Country Life*, 6 November 1915

Cartwright-Hignett, E., *Lili at Aynhoe* (1989)

Chambers, William, *A Dissertation on Oriental Gardening* (1772, reprinted London, 1972)

Christie's, Sale Catalogue, *Great Tew Park*, 27-29 May 1987

Christie's, *Catalogue of Books from the Library of Matthew Boulton and his Family*, 12 December 1986, lot 94

Demidowicz, George, *The Soho Inudstrial Buildings* (forthcoming)

Dick, Malcolm (ed.), *Matthew Boulton, a Revolutionary Player* (Birmingham, 2009)

Dickinson, H.W., *Matthew Boulton* (Cambridge 1936, republished Leamington Spa, 1999)

Doty, Richard, *The Soho Mint & the Industrialization of Money* (Smithsonian Institution, 1998)

Goodison, N., *Matthew Boulton: Ormolu* (London, 2002)

Hunt, J.D. and Willis, P. (eds), *The Genius of the Place* (London, 1975)

Hyams, Edward, *Capability Brown and Humphry Repton* (London, 1971)

Jacques, David, *Georgian Gardens, The Reign of Nature* (1983)

Jones, Peter, *Industrial Enlightenment: Science, Technology and Culture in the West Midlands, 1760-1820* (Manchester, 2009)

Kitz, Norman and Beryl, *Pains Hill Park* (Cobham, 1984)

Loggie, Val, 'Picturing Soho' in Mason, Shena (ed.), *Matthew Boulton: Selling what all the World Desires* (London, 2009)

Mason, Shena, *The Hardware Man's Daughter: Matthew Boulton and his 'Dear Girl'* (Chichester, 2005)

Mason, Shena (ed.), *Matthew Boulton: Selling what all the World Desires* (London, 2009)

Mason, William, *The English Garden, a Poem* (1783, reprinted New York, 1982)

Morriss, R.K., *Soho House, Handsworth, The Home of Matthew Boulton*, Hereford Archaeology Series 90 (1990)

Murray, Adam, *General View of the Agriculture of the County of Warwick* (1818)

Phillp, John, *Album of Sketches and Watercolours at Soho*, c.1790-99 (Birmingham Museums & Art Gallery)

Price, Uvedale, *Essays on the Picturesque* (London, 1810)

Schofield, R.E., *The Lunar Society of Birmingham* (Oxford, 1963)

Uglow, Jenny, *The Lunar Men* (London, 2002)

Uglow, Jenny, *A Little History of British Gardening* (London, 2004)

Whateley, Thomas, *Observations on Modern Gardening* (1772, reprinted New York 1982)

Index

Numbers in **bold** refer to illustrations

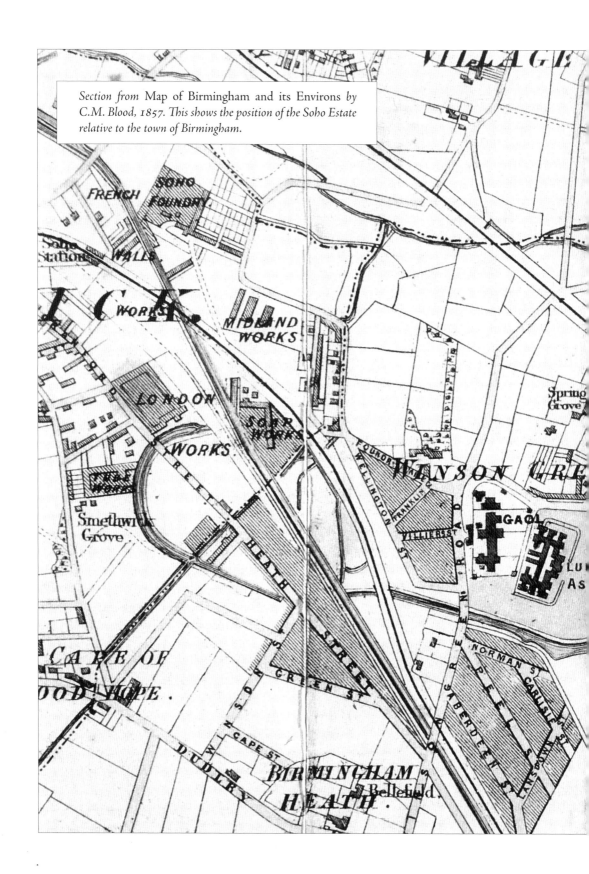

Section from Map of Birmingham and its Environs by C.M. Blood, 1857. This shows the position of the Soho Estate relative to the town of Birmingham.